PEACE AND DISPUTED SOVEREIGNTY

Reflections on Conflic Terri

Friedrich Kratochwil,
Project Director

Paul Rohrlich
Harpreet Mahajan

Columbia University
Institute of War and Peace Studies

Summer 1985

UNIVERSITY
PRESS OF
AMERICA

LANHAM • NEW YORK • LONDON

Copyright © 1985 by

University Press of America,® Inc.

4720 Boston Way
Lanham, MD 20706

3 Henrietta Street
London WC2E 8LU England

Library of Congress Cataloging in Publication Data

Kratochwil, Friedrich V.
  Peace and disputed sovereignty.

  Includes bibliographies and index.
    1. Boundary disputes.   2. Territory, National.
  3. Boundary disputes—Case studies.   4. Territory,
  National—Case studies. I. Rohrlich, Paul.
  II. Mahajan, Harpeet.   III. Columbia University.
  Institute of War and Peace Studies.   IV. Title.
  JX4111.K72   1985   341.4'2   85-91271
  ISBN 0-8191-4953-5 (alk. paper)
  ISBN 0-8191-4954-3 (pbk. : alk. paper)

Co-published by arrangement with the
Institute of War and Peace Studies,
Columbia University

TABLE OF CONTENTS

FOREWORD   v

INTRODUCTION   vii

     PART I

Ch. 1 Boundaries, Borders, and Disputed Sovereignty   3

Ch. 2 Patterns of Conflict   25

     PART II

     CASE STUDIES:
1 The Falkland/Malvinas Dispute   51
2 Ethiopia-Somalia Dispute   59
3 The Soviet-Japanese Territorial Dispute:
   The "Northern Territories"   65
4 Beagle Channel Dispute   71
5 US vs. Canada: The Gulf of Maine   79
6 Ecuador-Peru Dispute   85
7 The Aegean Sea Dispute   93
8 Arctic and Antarctica   101

     Part III

     CONCLUSION: Practical Applications   117

     A Methodological Note   137

     APPENDIX I: Contemporary Disputes   139

     INDEX   155

     About the Authors   159

iii

FOREWORD

The Falkland Islands War caught the world by surprise. It demonstrated how imperfectly we understand the dynamics of such long-existing but low-level disputes and their potential for ending in violent conflict. This led many people to ask about still unresolved but similar territorial or boundary disputes among neighboring states and about ways of promoting their peaceful settlement. Among those who promptly asked these questions was Earl Osborn who commissioned the present study, which was carried on under the auspices of the Institute of War and Peace Studies of Columbia University. We gratefully acknowledge both his perception for the need for the study and for his financial support. That support has enabled Friedrich Kratochwil and his associates to produce Peace and Disputed Sovereignty: Reflections on Conflict over Territory.

New York City
June 1985

Warner R. Schilling
Director
Institute of War and Peace Studies
Columbia University

v

INTRODUCTION

The Falkland Islands War is a classic case of a smoldering and intermittently dormant dispute among neighboring states suddenly bursting into the flame of violent conflict. Overlapping claims to territory and disagreement over the location of boundaries and the range of permitted transborder activity give rise to such cases of 'disputed sovereignty.' In the aftermath of the conflict over the Falkland (or Malvinas) Islands, this study is meant to answer four questions, viz.,

1. What other as yet unresolved cases of disputed sovereignty are there at the present time and what is their apparent potential for ending in violent conflict?

2. Under what circumstances are border disputes likely to escalate into violent conflict? Is there a pattern that distinguishes border conflicts from other types of conflicts?

3. How and when can such disputes be settled peacefully without third-party intervention on the basis of mutual acceptance of a common normative framework?

4. What is the role that third parties may play in achieving a peaceful settlement?

To answer these questions several research projects were undertaken. One was a survey conducted among the missions in New York of all UN members. Each mission received a letter and questionnaire about existing territorial and boundary disputes. These letters were followed up by personal calls and/or interviews when the mission had either indicated the existence of a dispute or had not reacted to our query. Instances of disputes turned out to be surprisingly numerous, and many are of long standing. The table in the Appendix I summarizes the findings of our survey which was completed in Spring 1985.

The second project was more conceptually oriented. We sought to clarify key concepts such as boundary, frontier, sphere of influence, etc. These concepts show similarities as well as differences in the way they distinguish different systems of interaction. Aside from definitional questions it soon became clear that a more thorough inquiry was required than the traditional investi-

vii

gation of boundary demarcation and delineation or of the issues surrounding "title" to territory. Many disputes arise out of historical claims or ethnic aspirations of a group that has been separated by a boundary even when neither the location nor the legal title to a particular territory is uncertain. For this reason we chose the term "border" dispute as an integrating concept which comprises classical boundary issues such as location of the demarcation line and title to territory as well as irredentist or historical claims.

Given these preliminary decisions the question of an adequate conceptual framework arose. We soon came to the conclusion that only by looking at the exchanges which boundaries regulate and by examining the changes in the type and intensity of these exchanges could an adequate framework for further research be developed. Rather than limiting the inquiry to legal and historical categories, the focus on exchanges and social relationships mediated by boundaries established the importance of three types of relations. There was first the issue of how the unit (state) related to the "environment" (understood as a symbol standing for all natural and social features); second, when significant "others" emerge through the break-up of the "environment" and are then recognized either as subordinate "clients" or as "co-equals," a new distinct type of inter-unit relationships comes into being. Finally, connected with these developments but analytically distinct, is the third type of relationship, i.e. the relation the "center" of a unit establishes with its "periphery." Thus, it is of great significance whether a "boundary" denotes exclusivity in terms of social and political organization, or whether it is compatible with personal and politically salient relations transcending the boundary (e.g., personal fealty in the Middle Ages). Similarly, it is important to know whether the boundary is conceptualized in terms of a line clearly marking off exclusive spheres of jurisdiction or whether it is seen as a broad zone in which the influence of the center comes to an end somewhere and perhaps overlaps with that of another "center" (e.g., the classical conception of imperial "frontiers").

It is the task of the first chapter of our study to provide a conceptual analysis of key terms such as boundary, border, frontier etc. Furthermore, a historical and comparative inquiry into the function of imperial frontiers and the concept of boundaries in an evolving international system provides the background and justification for the typology of border disputes which guided this study.

A third research project was geared towards a clearer recognition of the conflict patterns connected with border disputes arising from overlapping territorial claims. This required, above all, a clearer understanding of the conditions of escalation and de-escalation of conflicts. In using a common data bank of conflicts in the post-war era we sought to identify factors that make an eventual peaceful settlement of such disputes more (or less) likely, such as duration of the dispute, casualties suffered, alignment patterns. A more conceptual approach dealt with the stages of escalation and de-escalation, identifying crucial turning points in the dynamics of such disputes. Furthermore, a typology of third-party involvement in border disputes was developed. The role of implicit third parties (i.e. when normative frameworks help the parties in settling their differences) and of explicit third parties (mediation, adjudication) is discussed in the light of bargaining theory and the historical record. The terms "implicit" and "explicit third party" are adopted from Michael Barkun's fundamental study of international law and its role in mediating conflict in a decentralized authority system.[1] Chapter 2 of this study consequently investigates these problems dealing with patterns of conflict and types of border disputes.

At this point the reader might benefit from a closer investigation of some case studies. Eight such studies, which were conducted largely for heuristic reasons, form Part II of this study. They were chosen with regard to their representativeness of certain types of conflict: boundary demarcation vs. territorial claims, disputes involving developed states vs. those involving developing states, and those between powerful and weak states. We have not sought to make specific recommendations on "how to resolve" particular conflicts. Rather our studies are meant to help identify methods available for conflict resolution if and when both parties involved want to settle the dispute. Testing any of these suggested methods of course involves active diplomacy and is beyond our capabilities. Readers less interested in details can go directly to Part III, entitled "Conclusion: Practical Applications."

The conclusion tries to tie together the major theoretical arguments and to apply the insights gained from the case studies to the resolution of disputes. Here our concern centered on the role and involvement of third parties in facilitating the settlement of disputes. Although we are interested in the practical aspects of bargaining and conflict theory we want neither to suggest that our findings make every dispute susceptible to a settlement nor to claim that we can "predict" when and how any particular dispute is bound to escalate (or de-escalate). Our aim is more modest. Given that the escalation and de-escalation of disputes depends upon the choices of the contending parties, we seek to identify certain turning points in the evolution of conflicts. We may then suggest certain measures and strategies that are likely to lead to a settlement if the parties involved are disposed to settle even at the cost of making concessions rather than continue or increase hostilities. Thus knowing the opportunities and the conditions that made settlement of some important disputes possible contributes significantly to a clarification of choices and to a selection of de-escalatory strategies in situations where it appears difficult or impossible to reestablish control and to proceed in a deliberate fashion.

In this context we should make our value preferences explicit. For the purpose of this study we assume that uncoerced settlements based on agreement and on mutual recognition of rights is preferable to the (coerced) imposition of a "solution." This value preference results from the argument that boundaries not only separate but also link people by mediating their exchanges. Thus, while an "imposed" solution might under special circumstances -- such as great power differential between the disputants -- prevent a conflict from escalating, it is only the acceptance of principles which are to govern the exchanges between the countries that leads to the stability and finality of a settlement. To that extent freely accepted obligations and mutual recognition of the other's interests usually make for better relations and more unproblematic exchanges than coerced compliance with certain "facts of life."

Part III also contains an appendix reflecting the empirical side of the study. As we have already indicated, this appendix is based on a survey of all United Nations missions. It portrays the universe of contemporary disputes among states regarding boundaries and territories. Letters inquiring about currently pending disputes, what states they involve, and the basis for their claims were sent to all countries that maintain a mission to the UN and to the two Korean observer missions and the Swiss observer's office.[2] We inquired if their state had any: (a) unresolved territorial claims, (b) ambiguously demarcated boundaries, and (c) possible claims to resources or unclaimed territory such as the continental shelf or Antarctica which might conflict with another state's claims. We then asked what measures had been taken to resolve the dispute such as recourse to an international boundary commission, bilateral talks, or other means. One month later, follow-up letters and telephone calls were made urging a response from those missions which had not as yet responded. Several of the missions, for the sake of the public record, would only respond verbally and the same questions were then asked in interview format.

In reporting the responses in Appendix I, information contradictory to that reported by the state itself, either from public record, or another state's claim, is also recorded. Any issue that had been a policy consideration over the past three years was classified as "active" and all other claims as "passive." If a country did not respond, we noted it as "no response."

We want to thank all those in the many UN missions who gave their time and expertise through interviews and research materials. Appendix I and the Case Studies could not have been prepared without their co-operation. We regret that the time and resources of the project did not allow us to pursue more case studies in great detail and to use all the materials offered to us.

The members of the Institute of War and Peace Studies, particularly its Director, Warner R. Schilling, Louis Henkin, Roger V. Hilsman, John G. Ruggie, Oscar Schachter, and Jack Snyder provided valuable criticisms for which we are very grateful. We also owe a debt of gratitude to William T. R. Fox who was kind enough to read earlier drafts; from his suggestions and wisdom we benefitted greatly. Michael Galligan provided invaluable editorial assistance. Anna Hohri expertly shouldered the administrative burden of the project. Errors of facts and judgment are exclusively ours.

NOTES

1. Michael Barkun, <u>Law Without Sanction</u> (New Haven: Yale University Press, 1968).
2. To avoid duplication we did not seek information from the Byelorussian and Ukrainian missions.

PART I

Chapter I

BOUNDARIES, BORDERS AND DISPUTED SOVEREIGNTY

I

Those who make the future do not write on a clean slate. If the potentials for avoiding unnecessary violent conflict in the world's unresolved territorial disputes are to be realized, the marks on the slate must be studied with care. 'Territory' and 'boundary' are words freighted with historic meanings and those meanings vary from age to age, from culture to culture, and from situation to situation. Our search for methods of avoiding more Falkland Islands-type wars is, in the first instance, a search for those meanings. As with yellow fever, cures for the disease may be found far from the site of the epidemic.

Three quarters of a century ago, in his Romanes lectures[1], the British statesman Lord Curzon called boundaries the "razor's edge on which hang suspended the modern issues of war and peace, of life or death to nations."[2] Thus, just as the safeguarding of one's home is the most important concern of the private citizen, so the security of defined borders is the precondition of the existence and enjoyment of political autonomy in a society of states. Since the extension of the European state system to the rest of the world, the possession of territory has been the precondition for the exercise of legitimate political authority on the international level. Furthermore, the identification of the "self" with one's own national group often results in a territorial claim in order to protect one's own "way of life" and thus generates a spirit of nationalism: nations must have states and states must be nations. 'Territory' is no longer a purely administrative concept employed to delineate spheres of state authority; instead, it is directly associated with the core values which link individuals to their larger community.

Legal vs. Functional Approaches

Technically speaking, disputes over the geographic extent of a state's sovereignty entail two sets of legal problems. "Territorial" questions address the mode of acquiring title (discovery, occupation, cession etc.). "Boundary" questions in the narrower sense address issues concerning the demarcation and administration of specific "lines" which delineate exclusive spheres of jurisdiction between adjacent "states." From our short remarks above, however, it is clear that a wholly technical approach will leave out

3

many of the most interesting tensions arising out of the separa-
tions which boundaries impose. Thus, it is essential to analyze
the types of and/or inhibitions to exchanges and to the mediation
of social relationships worked by boundaries and not just the
location of the boundary and the title to territory. Any "right"
underlying the conception of "title," after all, is a socially
respected claim and thereby dependent upon a certain normative
framework by which social exchanges are mediated.

Three important implications follow. First, the "bundling of
rights" with which we associate the idea of "territorial sovereignty" is only one out of many possible ways to accommodate conflicting uses of certain areas.[3] As the present Draft Convention
of the Law of the Sea[4] illustrates, a variety of legal regulations are possible to achieve this end. Second, a closer examination of arrangements involving overlapping zones of jurisdiction
is useful for analyzing conflict patterns arising out of "border"
disputes. Although overlapping zones of jurisdiction (Continental
Shelf, Exclusive Economic Zone and free navigation) can be most
easily established in unsettled zones which have not been hereto-
fore allocated on an exclusive basis (terra nullius), a similar
unbundling of "sovereign" rights has been one of the more interesting features of managing the international system in the 19th
century. The neutrality "imposed" on Belgium and Switzerland as
well as the various zones of influence, buffer states, suzerainties and other devices by which the European "Great Powers" attempted to manage conflict in Europe and the rest of the world
must be studied. Third, aside from its historical relevance, the
study of border disputes and special regimes can indicate possible
"solutions" to contemporary problems of disputed sovereignty and
methods by which resulting conflicts can be prevented from escalating.

Thus, while this study does not offer an extensive survey of
the history of such problems, it uses a conceptual framework which
has been strongly influenced by the historical developments that
shaped the form and function of boundaries between modern states.

If we distinguish imperial borders from those of the modern
states system for instance, we can better understand the varying
functions of boundaries in mediating exchanges. In studying the
"genesis" of the modern 'disputed sovereignty problematique,' we
also see that three types of relationships take on particular importance. There is first the inter-state or unit-to-unit relation,
i.e., exchanges mediated through boundaries between "sovereign"
and therefore "equal" actors. But these relations are in turn con-
ditioned by a second set of relationships, i.e., the way in which
the political centers relate to their "periphery" or, in the language of international law, the relationship between the "federal"
state and its component parts. The legal formulation, however,
crystallizes at a relatively late date a much more fluid connec-

tion. In this context the question of who administers the boundary and maintains it is as relevant as who can "bind" the unit through treaties with other "units." It is also significant whether overlapping membership in different units is possible. During the feudal period in European history, for instance, a territorially-based system was compatible with overlapping personal jurisdiction. Third, there is the relationship between the unit and "others" who are not granted equal status. Here, "natural" boundaries serve as separating devices as well as locations for relations with "barbarian" tribes in the "outer darkness." Further issue areas under this rubric include transborder resource regimes where exploitation of resources according to territorial ownership is unfeasible or problematic. The use and damming of water for the generation of electricity and the joint management of fish stock are relevant examples.

While these analytical distinctions are useful in categorizing particular border disputes, we suggest that these distinctions are also useful for a more historically oriented investigation that tries to follow the evolutionary patterns of boundaries. For instance, if it could be shown that empires have a particular and distinct way of relating to "outsiders" by treating them as part of the "environment" rather than as equal political entities, this may have some specific implications for the other two relationships. The archetypical example is the Roman Empire which had only unequal relations with entities outside the empire. If significant interdependencies exist between these three sets of relationships, then a change in one should be of consequence for the other two. Rather than assuming that boundaries always "mean" the same when one social-political unit interacts with another, one must make an empirical enquiry about the type of exchanges actually involved.

In the following discussion, the importance of the three types of relationships is established through an inductive study of historical examples. The well-researched history of the Mongols who changed in historic times from a nomadic to a territorially based social organization provides materials for a case study of the various meanings of "territoriality" in tribal and non-tribal societies. Furthermore, the relationship of the Mongols to the Chinese empire which also underwent significant concomitant changes provides additional insights for the relations between imperial powers and "outsiders." Significant similarities between the Roman and British policies in frontier areas and the Chinese treatment of outsiders corroborates the hypothesis that boundaries, far from always mediating the same type of exchanges, have considerably different functions in empires and in a state system of sovereign equals.

Along with a difference in function went a difference in methods of conflict management, as the operations of the international system during the 19th century demonstrate. These methods

5

differed depending upon whether the issues concerned the European state system (inter-unit relations) or the "colonial world." The latter was characterized by the interaction effects of "imperial relations" (between the natives and the colonial power) and the danger of direct clashes among the European powers in the colonies. While the principle of territorial sovereignty in Europe seemed compatible with territorial divisions or with imposed "neutrality," a much greater variety of instruments were available to European powers in order to manage their potentially conflicting interests in the colonial world. For this purpose "spheres of interest" or influence, suzerainties, condominia, etc. were designed only to be swept away by the new power centers that developed during the emancipation of the colonial world and that insisted on the extension of territorial sovereignty to their territories. However, since many of the old demarcations of spheres resulted in modern "boundaries," a short discussion of the conditions giving rise to various boundary problems is not only of historical interest but of direct relevance to our considerations.

From these initial remarks the plan of the chapter follows. In the next section the discussion will focus on territorial rights and investigate the several meanings of this term in a variety of social organizations. The Mongol case study and the examples of Roman and British border policy are then described so as to highlight the differences between imperial and state boundaries. From here we can trace the evolution of the modern concept of territoriality by investigating fundamental turning points in the development of the three relationships outlined above.

The third section takes up the relation between various types of "boundaries" and instruments for managing conflict in the two-tiered international system during the 19th century. While sovereign territoriality did not leave much room for expansion and therefore had only changing coalitions, territorial adjustments, and neutralization as means of balancing interests, more flexible means of establishing influence could be imposed on the "unequal" colonial world. Thus, a strikingly different pattern of conflict management can be seen in the various "border" agreements that emerged in this setting.

The theoretical considerations developed in the sections II and III provide us with criteria for classifying various border disputes in section IV of this chapter. Furthermore, this typology also allows for a more precise determination of the scope of this study and for the selection of several "cases" which are typical of each type of dispute. This in turn prepares the ground for a discussion of patterns of border conflict which is taken up in the next chapter.

II

Territoriality and the Social Formation of States

Contemporary social science commonly distinguishes between a community based on kinship and one built upon the recognition of mutual rights subject to a common law within a given territory.[5] The study of the historical change from kinship groups to larger, hierarchically-organized associations based on territoriality has led to a distinction between "primitive" and "civilized" (or advanced) societies according to their level of social formation[6], i.e. the type of "rights" to the land the group has and the organizational means by which these rights are protected. However, the dichotomy between tribal and territorial communities is both empirically and conceptually problematic.[7] After all, even nomads do not wander aimlessly without fixed territory.

> The primitive nomad who depends for survival on what he can find...must know the territory in which he roams: locale of water holes, where certain plants grow, the habit of game etc. Thus each nomadic band establishes rights over the territory within which it migrates although its members may visit bands of other territories.[8]

In such nomadic communities the right to move prevails over the right to camp and "ownership means in effect the title to a cycle of migration."[9] Owen Lattimore has studied the implications of these forms of allocating territorial use-rights for the social formation in the case of the Mongols.[10] He traced the change in ways of using territory from the common use of tribally owned land administered by a prince (who allotted the use of pastures to different families and maintained the cycle of migration through loose alliances with other notables) to the establishment of fixed private ownership through the introduction of the monastic rule of Lamaism. The social consequences were startling.

The original Mongol tribes were never static since disputes over the right of movement led to the splitting and coalescence of small clan-like groups. This allowed an exceptional leader like Djinghis Khan to amass members in his tribe who had fled from their abusive or ineffective overlords and sought his protection and to hold sway over the largest portion of the earth's land area governed by any ruler in the world's history. Fundamental changes in the balance of power could be effected through this gathering of a leader's following.

The allocation of fixed property on the other hand prevented the process of agglomeration and led to the parcelling and repartitioning of tribal territory.

7

Dispute over boundaries and jurisdictions that the tribal society itself would have settled by the special tribal form of war (which consisted in summoning extra followers in order to claim wider cycles of migrations and more pastures), were now settled by compromise, and the sovereign instead of permitting one claimant to defeat the other and take over his following, made both of the contenders equal princes with diminished territories.... The new allocation of fixed boundaries, held fast by temple property in addition to the overlord's decree, brought the old transfer of allegiance under a new ruling and made it a new crime -- not desertion from the tribal lord but flight from the tribal territory. The migrant who thus left his lawful territory became a vagrant and as such was returnable on demand by the tribe into whose territory he had entered.[11]

The emphasis on fixed property first introduced by Lamaist monasteries led to further important internal as well as external changes. The former tribal constitutions emphasized mobility and forbade the digging of wells and intensive agriculture in order to adjust the Mongol "way of life" to the steppe rather than to the marginal areas which could have sustained a mixed form of economy. Exclusive property titles, however, led to the ascendancy of wealth over mobility and drew the Mongols closer to China through trade. This development brought them under the influence of the Manchus. Virtually all of the Mongols became their vassals, especially when China successfully intervened in church affairs and divided Northern from Western Mongols.

Most Western travellers in the 19th century commented on the more peaceful character of the once formidable Mongol people; both Chinese official writings and Western observers attributed this development to the teaching of Lamaism. Matters were, however, a bit more complicated: some of the bloodiest wars between Northern and Western Mongols had been conveniently neglected in these accounts.

What had really come to pass was that church property in buildings and land reinforced the secular policy of assigning fixed territories to tribes and their princes, thus defeating the mobility inherent in steppe pastoralism, which formerly had compensated for the abuse of power by chieftains through the degree in allegiance allowed to commoners.[12]

Lamaism had not only divided the Mongols and broken their ability to invade the Chinese empire but the settlements following the introduction of fixed property abolished the mobility which

8

had been one of the strategic assets for raiding the border. The development of "territoriality" in the new sense made a more fixed relationship with China necessary. Unable to unite and to maintain an independent basis of power, the Mongols became "suzerains" of the Manchu emperors. Similar arrangements could be found all along the Chinese "frontier" and it was only the clash with Russia that made a more precise definition of the relationship involved with the suzerains vis-a-vis Russia necessary. "Territoriality" again changed its meaning as the boundary mediated a different type of exchange.

The Treaty of Peking (1860) between Russia and Imperial China was an important step in this direction. It fixed the boundary as "following the mountains, great rivers and the present lines of Chinese permanent pickets." This delimitation still left a substantial part of the Sinkiang region on the Chinese side, but the Imperial Government did not decide to include Siankiang formally in the Chinese Empire until 1884. Afterwards, it still was treated as an "outer region" inhabited by "barbarians" over which largely indirect control was exercised. According to Geoffrey Wheeler, even until the 1940s Siankiang remained largely independent of governmental control by Peking.[13] The governors appeared to have conducted all pertinent internal as well as external policies.

Thus, although the western state system imposed a particular mode of territorial rule upon China's relationships with its clients and the "rest" of the world, the old social formation of China prevented the new "international boundary" from serving its function. Local leaders and Russian and Chinese clients made the attribution of the area to either "state" problematic even though there was formal international agreement on the location of boundaries. By the end of World War I the region was virtually a protectorate of the Czar. This relationship continued under Soviet rule and mineral exploitation passed nearly unchallenged to the Russians. The Sheng Shih-tsai regime broke in 1942 with the Soviets and switched allegiance back to Peking, but a Russian-inspired local rebellion reestablished Soviet influence. Only after the Chinese Revolution did the Kuldj regime friendly to Moscow disappear. The first treaties signed between the new Chinese People's Republic and Moscow protected Soviet interests in the area by setting up joint oil and mineral exploiting companies in which the Russians had a majority vote.[14] Stalin also used the same arrangement quite effectively in Eastern Europe in order to cement his political influence over Soviet client states. The arrangement with China continued until 1955.

The case of the Mongols has important implications for our study of border disputes. If boundaries are important because of their role in mediating exchanges, a closer look at the types of relationships mediated by boundaries will prove instructive. Most generally, boundaries are points of contact as well as separation between a social system and an "environment." As Niklas Luhmann remarked:

> [They] reduce the points of contact with the environment thus allowing the internal conditioning of various relations with the environment. Only where boundaries do exist, relations between system and environment can increase their complexity, their differentiation and their controlled mutability. Boundaries are permeable to causality; they only make sure that each causal process involves the entire system.[15]

Thus, the discussion concerning "natural boundaries" as well as the debate as to whether boundaries are supposed to separate peoples or provide for easy contact between them[16] involve important although poorly articulated issues.

The "natural boundary" of a mountain crest or watershed "separating" societies is only natural because these areas are usually sparsely populated and bereft of natural resources. Thus, exchange between societies or between a political system and its environment is minimized, and the potential for conflict is less, due to the lack of exchanges. But even the small number of exchanges with the environment largely depends upon the social formation of the societies involved. As Kingdon Ward remarked:

> ...obviously a pass of 15000 feet is nothing to a Tibetan who habitually lives at 12000 feet altitude. The Tibetan is not stopped by physical but climate barriers, and no boundary pillars are needed to make him respect these. His frontier is the verge of the grass land, the fringe of the pine forests, the 50 inch rainfall contour beyond which no salt is (until indeed you come to the sea) or the 75 percent saturated atmosphere. The barrier may be invisible; but it is a more formidable one to a Tibetan than the Great Hymalayan ranges. If he crosses it he must revolutionize his mode of life.[17]

Thus, it is important to distinguish between two types of exchanges: system-environment on the one hand, and system-other systems on the other. In addition one must consider how the center relates to the periphery, i.e. how and by what means the boundary is maintained. As long as the contacts with the people on the other side were rare,

> ...it was possible to manage...[relations] with a relatively low level of understanding and tolerance. On the other side of the borders were barbarian, primitives, nonbelievers, etc....who could be clas-

sified as part of the wild "environment" because not much came of them.... Long-range contacts were essentially reserved to higher strata and traders and supplied the system with "strange" objects and were thus only strengthening the awareness of a deep difference between system and environment. [18]

But when contacts increase and political and economic interdependencies are recognized, a differentiation between inter-system and system-environment relations arises. Exchanges between the system's units (states) are regulated by normative structures (even in cases of interstate violence). Thus, a "negative community"[19], i.e., one not united by a common purpose or vision of the "good life" but rather only by common practices and the mutual recognition of rights, comes into existence.[20] Boundaries become "lines" rather than zonal frontiers, although their exact demarcation may have to wait until adequate means of geodesy develop. The importance of the center-periphery relations and the task of boundary maintenance become visible. We see this pattern in the European context through the development of the European state system and the emergence of the classical conception of boundaries defining exclusive zones of jurisdiction. The Treaty of the Pyrenees between Spain and France (1659) set up a joint commission for deciding the exact boundary line, and this led to the demarcation of the first official boundary in the modern sense.[21] There were earlier efforts to demarcate "boundaries" with some precision (e.g., Philip le Bel's attempt in 1312 to determine boundaries of Flanders)[22], but because of the largely personalistic political organization of the time the significance of the demarcation was quite different. Under feudal rule, "loyalty" was owed, depending on circumstances, to different overlords simultaneously. Thus, although the limits of the realm were quite well known, there was a tendency to obfuscate the "boundaries" of the kingdom. Nobles made war on their own and had pretensions on domains in other realms. Interventions and counterinterventions were the order of the day, and "kingdoms" could not act like unitary "states."[23] Only exclusive "sovereignty" made defense and internal administration the primary and increasingly exclusive task of the central authorities. This development illustrates the complexity of the concept of "sovereignty." It denotes internal hierarchy as well as external equality. It captures the complexities involved in the new concept of boundaries in a system of multiple sovereignties.

The pattern of similarities and differences between boundaries in a state system and those developing in the frontier zones of empires is striking and shows the usefulness of analytically separating center-periphery relations from those of inter-system interactions, and system-environment exchanges. Although the Great Wall in China and the Roman limes appear to be cases of linear boundaries they are not boundaries in the modern sense. As Lattimore points out:

...the concept of a man-made Great Wall...was more a product of the kind of state created within [emphasis added] China than of the kind of pressure against China from the steppe. Naturally enough, it is the military aspect of the Great Wall that has commanded most attention, and this has distorted its historical significance.[24]

Considering the immense military strength of Ch'in at the end of the period of the warring states, the border changes of the Great Wall were neither very extensive, when compared to the territories of the former feudal kingdoms Ch'in had united, nor was there any imminent menace of Northern barbarians pressing inside. Most of the military threats came from the still unconquered south:

...the only wars against barbarians of the Inner Asian Frontiers were not wars of defense but clearing operations for the straightening of the new Ch'in Great Wall.... The true purpose of both wall building and road building had to do with stabilizing the conquests that had been made in China, and with setting to rights a new order of society.[25]

Thus the elimination of feudalism abolished the "cellular" structure of Chinese society, a pattern in which walled cities had dominated the surrounding countryside for long periods of time without giving rise to central institutions. The destruction of feudalism proceeded through the Ch'in's deliberate policy of exterminating the nobility and of converting the feudal serfs into peasants who owed rent to their overlord and taxes to the state. The noble could no longer use the serf as a soldier but was entitled to rent only; the peasant now could be approached directly by the state for taxes and conscripted labor without the intercession of the feudal lord. The defense of the boundaries became, in contrast to the situation prevailing under feudalism, a task of the central authorities and the boundaries served not to demarcate areas of competing jurisdiction on the basis of shared practices and mutual recognition of rights but to keep the "environment" safe through the establishment of clients and the control of trade.

Similarly, the Roman empire conceived the "limes" not as a boundary but as a stopping place where the potentially unlimited expansion of the pax Romana had temporarily come to a halt.[26] The political as well as administrative domain often extended far beyond the wall[27] -- certain Roman "castra" (military posts) have been found near Aberdeen far to the North of Hadrian's Wall -- and sometimes receded from it considerably. "Boundaries," i.e., legally relevant territorial distinctions, existed only in private legal relations where they governed property rights. But the ager publicus or public domain had no boundaries; it came somewhere to an end without any legally relevant line being specifiable. (The expression used was "fines esse.") The boundary was, therefore, essentially a floating zone within which tributary tribes as well as Roman legions with barbarian recruits were used to keep the peace.[28] Other barbarian tribes were to be slowly acculturated and integrated or to be subjected and suppressed. Caesar's political plan, expressed in his Commentaries [29] as well as in Plutarch[30], represents not only his personal political thinking but the policy consensus in Rome at least until the time of Commodus (180-192 A.D.) when the grandiose plans to conquer the world up to the "earth-surrounding ocean" were abandoned.

Caesar believed that there was a fundamental difference between the Gauls, somewhat acculturated by the Romans through frequent contact, and the Germanic tribes that were said to grow the fiercer the further they were removed from the Roman frontier.[31] For example, the powerful Suebes neither carried on trade with the Romans and the Gauls nor did they want to enter into regularized relations. Rather, they laid waste to a broad zone in order to isolate themselves from foreign influences.[32] Caesar concluded that the security of the Roman Empire required the subjection of isolated tribes that were not susceptible to transformation through contact into tributaries. Thus, before his assassination Caesar had prepared for a war against the Parthians. It was to include an expedition against Burebista and the Dacians on the lower Danube and then to proceed further north against the Germanic tribes.[33] Since Caesar did not know of the existence of the European (not to mention the Asian) part of Russia -- the Caspian Sea was assumed to be the enclosing northern ocean -- such plans would have indeed brought all the inhabited known world (with the exception of India) under Roman rule.[34] Attacks from the depth of the "unpacified" space, such as the Cimbric and Teutonic tribes had carried out, would have become impossible. Practically, Caesar's plans came to naught and Rome developed client relationships with the northern Germanic tribes which lasted until internal decay and the crushing defense burdens brought the imperial organization to its knees.

A closer look at client relationships as well as at the similarities and differences in managing inter-societal affairs in the state system is now appropriate.

III

Boundaries and the Management of the International System

The distinction introduced in the previous section between frontiers and boundaries and the orientation away from the classical boundary problems of "delimitation and demarcation" toward a broader view of the function of borders under conditions of vari-

13

ous social formations help clarify some issues of conflict management in international relations. Basically, two classes of techniques were available: one was the management of the various types of exchanges mediated by boundaries, and the other was the manipulation of the boundary location. The latter was typical of the European balance of power system, characterized by attempts to "preserve the equilibrium in Europe" through territorial divisions such as the division of Poland and territorial adjustments such as those at the Congress of Vienna.[35] The former was employed most consistently around the edges of the various European "empires" that subjected a "colonial world" to those empires. Institutions like buffers, protectorates, spheres of interest (or influence), suzerainties, neutral zones were commonly used in order to impose European rule on more or less recalcitrant "locals" and to manage potential conflicts with other expanding European powers.[36] Meanwhile, the institutions of "servitudes" and imposed "neutralization" also played a role within the European state system.

With the emancipation of the colonial areas many of the lines formerly marking off spheres of interest became hard and fast boundaries of successor "states" and some of the present boundary disputes result from such "spheric" agreements. The dispute between Ethiopia and Somalia and the Indian-Chinese boundary problem concerning the meaning and understandings underlying the McMahon line in Tibet (dividing Tibet in two spheres but acknowledging the "suzerainty" of China) are cases in point.[37] Nevertheless, some "parallels" or spheric boundaries such as the 49° parallel are still in existence and serve as functioning boundaries in the present world.

It would be interesting to inquire into the reasons why some meridians designed more as markers indicating agreements in principle for uncharted territory have become boundaries without engendering conflict while others have not. It seems that one or more of the following conditions helped to mitigate potential disputes. First, most of the astronomical boundaries still in existence are in deserts or polar regions. The maintenance of such lines can be explained in terms of the costs of demarcation in an uncharted and hostile environment. Second, straight lines persisted when the same colonial power gained possession of the adjacent territory which was once marked off as lying in some other power's spheres of influence. Former spheric demarcations therefore became internal administrative boundaries and only later, through state succession, an international boundary. The Egypt-Sudan, Tanzania-Kenya, and Botswana-South West Africa borders are cases in point. The acceptance of the 49° parallel as the boundary between Canada and the US has to be explained differently. Jefferson advocated this boundary in 1818 by pointing out that the proposed line had roots in early 18th century diplomacy. This proposal was acceptable to England also.

Most of the time, however, former demarcation lines marking off the spheres into which European power rivalry was projected, gave rise to more complicated arrangements. For instance, the treaty which established the Anglo-German sphere of influence in Africa in 1890 specifically provided for future adjustments in accordance with local requirements.[38] Consequently, the boundaries that emerged between Malawi, Tanzania, Uganda and Rwanda, Kenya and Tanzania show alterations (or are still in dispute).

The second method mentioned above, to impose a special regime rather than to move a boundary in the "frontier" zone, gave rise to patterns of interaction quite different from those between the sovereign territorial regimes characteristic of Europe. The Balkans represented in the 19th century a frontier zone in which Austrian, Russian and British influence met and in which the nominal power could not effectively deal with the challenges to the Turkish empire. Besides, Turkey was not considered a European state and was admitted to the rank of a "civilized" nation only after the Crimean War. Subsequent arrangements in the Balkans, therefore, resembled those of colonial areas. Capitulations that conferred jurisdiction over nationals living and working in a foreign country, leased zones, custom receiverships, etc. were management tools in order to come to terms with commercial penetration.

...[Such] capitulations or other allied arrangements existed at various times in Turkey, Egypt, Tunis, Morocco, Tangier, the Congo, Liberia, Madagascar, Siam, China and Japan. Uncertainity as to the legal and political status of an area, even where a single power is de facto...supreme, has proved a constant deterrent to investment and development.[39]

These problems led to attempts at strengthening foreign authority through political and legal means. On the lowest level of formalization is the "sphere of interest" either backed by formal or informal agreements among competitor states alone (when the locals do not matter) or by additional arrangements with the local authorities. A sphere of influence denotes, in Lord Curzon's words, "no exterior power but one may reassert itself in the territory so described."[40] Spheres of influence have therefore also been called "semi-suzerainties." Other arrangements such as the institution of a "protectorate" or (full) suzerainty or condominia had also developed. The tripartite condominium between Germany, Britain and the USA over Samoa lasted for a decade from 1889 on and the Anglo-French arrangements in Sudan and the New Hebrides represent similar arrangements.

Surveying the range of various "frontier" arrangements in 1945, Duncan Hall provided this rather surprising (but not exhaustive) set of mandates, international regimes, trusteeships, etc.

15

...reading from south to north, is as follows: the mandates (now trusteeships) of Ruanda-Urundi and Tanganyika; the Uganda Protectorate; rivalries and spheres of influence over Abyssinia; Eritrea, in turn Turkish, Egyptian, Italian, and now projected international trusteeship; rivalries of Britain and France over Egypt and the valley of the Nile culminating in the Fashoda incident; the condominium of the Sudan; the former condominiums and protectorate over Egypt; the neutralized and demilitarized Suez Canal, with its international regime; the mandates over Transjordan, Palestine, and Syria; the projected international trusteeship regime for Jerusalem; the checkered history of Alexandretta, in turn Turkish territory, League mandate, international regime, and again Turkish territory. As we shall see, the line of phenomena of the international frontier continues historically through Anatolia, along the straits, through the Balkans, and thence on to the Baltic and even to the Arctic.[41]

(See e.g., the discussion of the Spitzbergen treaty in the Arctic-Antarctica study.)

Finally, there was the arrangement of neutral zones or of a buffer state, allowing the "locals" considerable autonomy. The former often became unviable when local refugees or even brigands used the lack of a strong internal or external authority for their own purposes. The neutral zone between Britain and Germany separating the Gold Coast and Togo had to be abolished in 1899 for that reason. Neutral zones, i.e., areas without political authority, have been abolished in modern times as the exclusivity of territorial rule became more and more important. Thus, the neutral zone between Saudi Arabia and Iraq was abolished in 1981 by dividing the territory equally.[42]

A good example of the buffer state arrangement is the recognition of Afghanistan's role as a buffer which was supposed to separate British and Russian influence effectively. Having failed to impose imperial rule upon the resisting tribes and having experienced friction with another European power (Russia) which participated in "local politics," the British, with Russian consent, persuaded the Emir of Afghanistan to accept sovereignty over Vakhan. A curious extension of Afghan territory towards China was thereby created. In a similar vein, Siam, too was successful in defending its own autonomy against two direct interventions by becoming a "neutral" in the British-French contest in Indo-China.

As in the European context, neutralization depended upon Great power agreement and the inability or costliness of extending the imperial borders.[43] The usual precondition was that the ter-

16

ritory in question was effectively administered by some sort of "government" that could prevent easy penetration. Otherwise various client arrangements had to be developed in order to prevent either the excluded states from invading or, in case the border people were weakly organized, to prevent internal pressure (from colonists, traders, military careerists etc.) to involve the imperial state in further expansion at great cost. The social formation of the imperial state was therefore as important as that of the outer "barbarians" or tribes. Historical examples of such expansion through private activities are Cecil Rhodes and Luederitz in Africa, who extended British and German influence by forcing the governments to protect their private acquisitions. The debate concerning the "causes" of imperialism and the arguments that the "empire" does not "pay" are also familiar in this context. The acquisition of Texas in the American "frontier" context shows also the extensions of influence caused originally by private initiative.

The dynamics created by this clash of internal and external formation can be seen in England's policy in India. In the case of the British Northwest Frontier, London's policy vacillated between a "closed border" policy and a "forward policy." The closed border policy entailed the strict patrol by the British of the border, negotiations limited to the representatives of transborder societies, and British insistence on the right of supervising and controlling transborder affairs. This was usually accompanied by an otherwise non-interventionist stance toward "tribal affairs," punctuated by occasional punitive expeditions when the security of British India was threatened. The "forward policy" on the other hand -- exemplified by the Sandeman system of consultation and a more active intervention in "tribal" affairs -- consisted of arbitration and subsidies in order to keep the peace while not discouraging contacts between the "subjects" of the empire and the outsiders. [44]

This survey of the sources of border disputes in terms of the formation and function of boundary arrangements and the theoretical considerations derived from the survey make it possible to take the next step. That step is to state more precisely the scope of the present study.

IV

The Scope of the Present Study

Since border disputes are legion, some categories of disputes must be excluded in order to limit the universe of cases to those needed to preserve the theoretical (and thereby also practical) import of our study. Three formal criteria delimit the universe of cases whose conflict potential will be investigated:

17

1. The focus is on existing disputes. Historically important disputes are only of interest as far as they provide clues about the successful solution (or non-resolution) of the conflict.

2. Only disputes between established territorial units will be investigated. Conflicts arising out of the unfulfilled aspirations of a particular ethnic group are excluded. While it is obvious that such disputes are prone to conflict escalation they are really quite different from territorial and boundary disputes proper.

3. Cases are chosen and are studied in ways that illustrate _types_ of disputes. No comprehensive survey of existing territorial disputes between established territorial units is attempted and none of the disputes is described in greater detail than is needed to make clear the essential characteristics.

In this context a more fruitful strategy is to develop different models of disputes rather than to study each or many of them in great detail. The elaboration of ideal types helps not only to classify conflicts but also to highlight features that have theoretical import for the assessment of the conflict potential of any given dispute. Classifying boundary and border issues of disputed sovereignty in this way is not merely (or even primarily) a taxonomic task; it informs us, at least indirectly, about the likelihood and the conditions of an eventual settlement.

On the basis of the conceptual distinction above we want to distinguish the following types of disputes:

a) Territorial disputes -- disputes related to the social formation of the social systems in question and which deal with inter-system exchanges. Here historical arguments, ethnic and cultural similarities and strategic considerations variously serve as justifications for the boundary changes advocated.

b) Positional disputes -- those resulting from uncertainty as to the exact location of the demarcated boundary lines. To that extent these raise largely technical issues concerned with boundary-making (delineation, demarcation and enforcement), but the center-periphery dynamic may also come into play as the example

18

of the transformation of spheres into boundaries in the cases of Tibet and Sinkiang
illustrated.

c) Functional boundary disputes -- mainly those
involving the utilization of a transboundary
resource such as the waters of a boundary
river (or electric power generated by it). The
disaggregation of the concept of "sovereign
rights" over certain areas in favor of granting exclusive (or competing access) to particular resources has been one of the main issues
at the Law of the Sea Conference and an important class of dispute is likely to arise from
the unsettled character of the present Draft
Convention concerning these resource zones.
Similar problems can be expected in the case
of Antarctica, as the special case study will
show.

Representative case studies are included from each of the
three dispute categories -- territorial, positional, and functional. In this context two points should be borne in mind. Within
each category the selection of a particular dispute was based on
an assessment of the potential for armed conflict and its relation
to world politics on the one hand and on the availability of historical and other background material on the other. While the suggested research strategy of developing "ideal types" and categorizing existing disputes accordingly is heuristically fruitful,
actual disputes may show features from more than one type. This
will become clear from the reading of the "case studies" in Part
II.

An attempt has been made to include disputes among developing
states, among advanced developed states, and between developed and
developing states. A further consideration was the intra-bloc vs.
inter-bloc nature of the dispute. Bloc rivalries may be muted (due
to the strategic considerations) on the one hand, while the potential for conflict as a factor exacerbating tension may be higher
on the other.

Territorial disputes examined are: the Ethiopian-Somali conflict over the Ogaden region; the Argentine-British strife regarding the Falkland (or Malvinas) and South Georgia islands; the
Japanese-Soviet dispute over several islands north of Hokkaido,
the so-called "Northern Territories." The positional dispute cases
selected for study are the Ecuador-Peru conflict concerning their
border in the Amazon basin, the Chilean-Argentinian conflict over
the Beagle Channel, and the US-Canada dispute delimiting the territorial sea in the Gulf of Maine. Functional disputes chosen are
those revealed in a study of the Arctic and the Antarctic regimes,

19

and that over continental shelf between Turkey and Greece.

In those cases in which the territorial, positional and/or functional issues cannot be easily delinked, the dispute has been classified with regard to the root cause of the dispute. For example, while the lack of a distinct boundary between Somalia and Ethiopia has led to violent conflict, it is the dispute over the territory through which the boundary runs that prevents the resolution of the border issue and which leads us to classify it as a territorial dispute. Conversely, while Argentina and Chile dispute the sovereignty of the Lenox, Nueva, and Picton Islands in the Beagle Channel, it is the border-line lying in the Channel that categorizes the matter as positional.

So much for the categorization of disputes so as to elaborate "ideal types" of disputes over sovereignty. We now examine the context of the disputes and the conditions for conflict resolution. Our focus is necessarily on the means of muting or mediating these disputes so as to prevent violent conflict. In this respect, we have found the role of "third parties" to be particularly interesting.

NOTES

1   Lord Curzon, Romanes Lectures 1907, Frontiers (Oxford: Clarendon, 1907).

2   Ibid., p. 7.

3   For a short discussion of the importance of "sovereignty" as such an internal as well as external bundle of rights see John Gerard Ruggie, "Continuity and Transformation in the World Polity," World Politics, vol. 35 (January 1983), pp. 261-285, as well as the extensive literature quoted in this essay.

4   For a discussion of the some of the new concepts such as "Exclusive Economic Zone" etc. see below; for a text of the UN Draft Convention on the Law of the Sea see International Legal Materials, vol. 21 (November 1982).

5   See, e.g., Maine's and Morgan's work on kinship or "primitive" societies. H.M. Maine, Ancient Law (London: John Murray, 1866); Lewis Morgan, Ancient Society or Researches in the Lines of Human Progress from Savagery through Barbarism to Civilization (New York: H. Holt, 1877). For a critique of this dichotomy see Robert Lowie, Primitive Society (London: Routlege, Kegan Paul, 1949).

6   By social formation we mean the way in which the division of labor is organized in a society and protected by a system of

rights.
7   See, e.g., I. Schapera, Government and Politics of Tribal Societies (London: Watts, 1956); and Lucy Mair, Primitive Government (London: Penguin, 1962). The latter stresses the emergence of cross-cutting cleavages and the emergence of politics arising out of contiguity.

8   T.S. Murty, Frontiers: A Changing Concept (New Delhi: Palit and Palit, 1978), p. 50.

9   See, e.g., the extensive discussion of "nomadism" in Owen Lattimore, Inner Asian Frontiers of China (Boston: Beacon Press, 1951), Ch. 4, at pp. 66ff.

10 Owen Lattimore, The Mongols of Manchuria (New York: John Day, 1934).

11 Lattimore, Inner Asian Frontiers, op. cit., pp. 80, 90.

12 Ibid., p. 97.

13 For a general discussion see, Surya Sharma, International Boundary Disputes and International Law (Bombay: Tripathi, 1976), pp. 194ff.; and Geoffrey Wheeler, "Siankiang and the Soviet Union," The China Quarterly (November-December 1963), pp. 57ff.

14 See, P.P. Karan, "The Sino-Soviet Border Dispute," Journal of Geography, vol. 63 (1964), pp. 216-222.

15 Niklas Luhmann, "Territorial Borders as System Boundaries" in Raimondo Strassoldo and Giovanni Delli Zotti, eds., Cooperation and Conflict in Border Areas (Milano: Franco Angeli, 1982), pp. 235-245, at p. 236.

16 See, e.g., T.F. Holdich, Political Frontiers and Boundary Making (London: MacMillan, 1916).

17 Kingdon Ward, "Explorations on the Burma-Tibet Frontier," Geographical Journal, vol. 80 (1932), pp. 465-83, as quoted in J.R.V. Prescott, Boundaries and Frontiers (London: Croom Helm, 1978), p. 108.

18 Luhmann, "Territorial Borders as System Boundaries," op. cit., p. 238.

19 We use the term "negative community" for denoting the situation in which there is an agreement on common practices and rights but not on common purposes. For a further discussion see, Terry Nardin, Law, Morality and the Relations of States (Princeton: Princeton University Press, 1983).

20 For the argument that the European state system depended upon a variety of conventions and institutional rules, see Maurice Keens-Soper, "The Practice of a State System" in Michael Donelan, ed., The Reason of States (London: Allen and Unwin, 1978), pp. 25-45.

21 Sharma, International Boundary Disputes, op. cit., p. 14.

22 Ibid.

23 For further discussions of this point see, Gianfranco Poggi, The Development of the Modern State (Stanford: Stanford University Press, 1978); and Joseph Strayer, On the Medieval Origins of the Modern State (Princeton: Princeton University Press, 1970).

24   Lattimore, Inner Asian Frontiers, op. cit., p. 434.
25   Ibid., p. 441.
26   This thesis has been put forward most eloquently by Paul de Lapradelle, La Frontière (Paris: Les Editions Internationales, 1928). For some important modifications of the Lapradelle thesis see Studien zu den Militaergrenzen Roms, Vortraege des 6. Internationalen Limes Kongresses in Sueddeutschland (Koeln-Graz: Boehlau Verlag, 1967).
27   See, e.g., the extensive discussion of Roman boundary arrangements in Franz Altheim, Niedergang der Alten Welt, (Frankfurt: Vittorio Klosterman, no date), Vol. II, Chs. 2 and 3.
28   Ibid., Ch. 4.
29   Julius Caesar, De Bello Gallico [Commentaries], John Warrington, trans. (New York: Dutton, 1953).
30   Plutarch, Vitae Caesarum [The Lives of the Caesars] (New York: Heritage Press, 1941), Ch. 58, 6.
31   See, e.g., his remarks "Germani multum ab hoc consetudine (Gallorum) differunt," Caesar, op. cit., Bk 6, 21, 1.
32   Caesar, De Bello Gallico, op. cit., Bk 4, 3, 1 & Bk 6, 23, 2.
33   For a discussion of Caesar's plans in Plutarch's record see Altheim, Niedergang der alten Welt, op. cit., pp. 22-28; Eduard Meyer, Caesars Monarchie und das Prinzipat des Pompaeius, (Stuttgart, Berlin: Cotta, 1919), p. 469.
34   Plutarch, Vitae Caesarum, op. cit., Caesar, 58, 6. On the (mistaken) geographic notions (which were probably derived from Poseidonios), see Altheim, Niedergang, op. cit., p. 26.
35   See, e.g. the various compensation schemes of the Congress of Vienna in Edward Gulick, Europe's Classical Balance of Power (Ithaca, New York: Cornell University Press, 1955), Ch. 9.
36   For a fundamental discussion along these lines see H. Duncan Hall, Mandates, Dependencies and Trusteeships (Washington, D.C.: Carnegie Endowment for International Peace, 1948), Ch. 1: The International Frontier.
37   See J.R.V. Prescott, H.J. Collier and D.F. Prescott, Frontiers of Asia and Southeast Asia (Melbourne : Melbourne University Press, 1977), Ch. 18.
38   Art. IV. See also the discussion in, K.C. McEwen, International Boundaries of East Africa (Oxford: Clarendon, 1971), pp. 178ff. See, e.g., the shift of the boundary at Lake Jipe from the shore to the middle was due to the work of a boundary commission in 1904-6 which modified the original agreement between Germany and Britain (1893). The new line became the modern Kenya-Tanzania boundary.
39   Duncan Hall, "The International Frontier," American Journal of International Law, vol. 42 (1948), pp. 42-65, at p. 45.
40   Lord Curzon, Frontiers, op. cit., p. 42.
41   Duncan Hall, "The International Frontier," op. cit., p. 44.
42   Alan J. Day, ed., Border and Territorial Disputes (Keesings, 1982), pp. 229-232.
43   For a discussion of the problems involved, see Cyril Black et

al., <u>Neutralization in World Politics</u> (Princeton, N.J.: Princeton University Press, 1968).

44   For a discussion of the British policy, see I. Coatman, "The North West Frontier Province and Trans-Border Country under the New Constitution," <u>Journal of the Royal Central Asian Society</u>, vol. 18 (July 1931), pp. 335-48; and C.E. Bruce, "The Sandeman Policy as Applied to the Tribal Problems of Today," <u>Journal of the Royal Central Asian Society</u>, vol. 19 (January 1932), pp. 45-67.

Chapter II

PATTERNS OF CONFLICT

I

Because territoriality is the organizing principle of the international system, boundary disputes have great potential for escalating into war. An attack on the territorial integrity of a state not only violates the basic rule of international law since the end of the World War II which prohibits the use of force in international relations. The legal exception of self-defense to this general prohibition frequently serves as an excuse to resort to violence. Border and boundary disputes at first glance seem to be the most obvious instances of zero-sum conflict in international relations and do not appear to be easily susceptible to peaceful settlement. One astute observer of such disputes has even concluded that the "use of coercion is still the principal feature of settling boundary disputes."[1]

The empirical evidence suggests a very different conclusion. First, as a survey conducted as part of this study shows, border and boundary disputes are quite frequent and, significantly, often of considerable duration (see Appendix I). Our universe of cases does not include several outstanding continental shelf delimitations which are likely to lead to further disputes as soon as some states (notably the People's Republic of China) decide to define their baselines.[2] Second, only a few of the disputes have led to large-scale violence, although sporadic acts or threats of force are not rare. Finally, many such disputes do get settled either explicitly through formal agreements or implicitly by being dropped from the international agenda. These results raise several interesting questions.

One, is there a pattern to border and boundary conflicts of disputed sovereignty which will distinguish them from other conflicts of interest? Two, how can the episodic character of these long-term conflicts be accounted for? Three, given the duration of many of the disputes, when can we be confident that a "settlement" has been reached, achieving the "stability and finality" of which the International Court of Justice spoke in the <u>Temple of Preah Vihear</u> case?[3] Four, under what circumstances are legal appeals or efforts at mediation most likely to succeed? Five, when are border and boundary disputes likely to escalate and end in "war" rather than in the sporadic acts of coercion mentioned above? Six, is the implication of functionalist theory correct when it implies

25

that the "unbundling" of exclusive territorial rights is likely to de-escalate conflicts because of the diminishing importance of national boundaries?

Specific functional agreements often do provide for the common and peaceful utilization of transborder resources. However, as the Arctic-Antarctic case study shows, it is questionable whether attempts to organize whole areas by means of functional regimes are viable if the parties do not agree by the same token to form robust common institutions with continuous upgrading of the institutional framework. Overlapping regimes, particularly when negotiated at different times, may create significant externalities quite apart from the difficulties which frequently emerge about the meaning and range of application of each one to an issue area.

These observations suggest the line of analysis in this chapter. We first consider some quantitative findings concerning boundary conflicts. Caution is in order considering the rather crude analysis of aggregate data, particularly when the universe of cases is not large enough to make "controls" for other factors possible. Thus, some of the most interesting relationships might disappear in the overall picture, as the famous example of the man who drowned in a basin that was on the average three feet deep teaches us. True, since R.L. Butterworth's Managing Interstate Conflict [4] lists only 310 interstate security conflicts for the period 1945-74 and of these only a restricted number resulted from territorial and boundary disputes, these criticisms could justifiably be made. Nevertheless, some interesting patterns emerge. Furthermore, the in-depth study of representative cases will take care of the interesting "hole" problem in the 3 feet deep basin. One of the following section analyses the problem of conflict escalation and settlement. Section four discusses the role of third parties and their contributions in bringing about peaceful resolutions of boundary conflicts. A short summary of the main arguments is provided in section five.

II

Border and Boundary Disputes: A Quantitative First Cut

As mentioned above, boundary disputes are surprisingly frequent and are of considerable duration, often oscillating between active and latent stages. Using R.L. Butterworth's data base, we can conclude that out of the 310 interstate security conflict cases in the period 1945-1974, 162 conflict cases occurred between bordering states and 66 cases had a clear border or boundary dispute component. Out of these 66 cases, 24 involved some military action. Taking casualties and duration as indicators of "seriousness" and cross-tabulating border and non-border conflicts, we obtain the results presented in Table I.

26

TABLE I

		NON-BORDER n	BORDER n	Total n
	None	33	9	42
PEOPLE	1-100	49	7	56
KILLED	101-1000	41	6	47
	1001-2000	13	2	15
	>2000	37	0	37
	Sum:	173	24	197
	<1 year	48	1	49
TIME	1-2 years	20	3	23
	2-3 years	16	2	18
	>3 years	86	18	106
	Sum:	173	24	197

Source: Butterworth, op.cit.

A somewhat surprising finding of these two tables is that although border conflicts tend to last longer than non-border conflicts, the number of people killed tends to be lower in the former. This indicates the relatively low intensity of most border
clashes, at least during the thirty years Butterworth surveyed,
since otherwise we should expect the number of fatalities to increase with time.

If we look at how the number of people killed affect the
chances of settlement, the following picture emerges. There is an
obvious relationship between settlement and a lack of fatalities;
only one out of nine conflicts involving no casualties had not
been settled. The duration of these conflicts does not seem to be
significant. Thus, while violence obviously aggravates a dispute
(or is an indicator of how serious it is, the small n does not
make a statistical control between these two hypotheses possible),
the length of a "smoldering" conflict appears to be of no significance (see Table II).

TABLE II

CONFLICT SETTLED

		No	Yes	Total
	<1 year	0	1	1
TIME	1-2 years	1	2	3
	2-3 years	0	2	2
	>3 years	9	9	18
	Sum:	14	10	24

TABLE II (contd.)

CONFLICT SETTLED

		No	Yes	Total n
	None	1	8	9
PEOPLE	1-100	4	3	7
KILLED	101-1000	3	3	6
	>1000	2	0	2
	Sum:	10	14	24

Source: Butterworth, op. cit.

Boundary disputes which are territorial in nature (i.e., which have in Butterworth's terms a strong "ethnic" component), are less likely to be settled (see Table III).

TABLE III

CONFLICT SETTLED

		No	Yes	Total
TERRITORIAL	1) No	4	9	13
[ETHNIC	2) Slight	1	4	5
CONFLICT]	3) Strong	5	1	6
	Sum:	10	14	24

Source: Butterworth, op. cit.

Similarly, Robert Mandel's analysis of Butterworth's data showed that territorial or ethnically motivated border conflicts are more severe than functional disputes about resources.[5]

Finally, there emerge surprising patterns concerning bloc membership and/or alignment. Somewhat counterintuitively, we find that shared bloc membership seems to inhibit settlement and non-alignment of the parties involved appears to make a settlement more likely (see Table IV).

This evidence plainly contradicts the conventional hegemony thesis according to which the bloc leader should be capable of muting or resolving differences in his bloc. The evidence suggests a much more complicated pattern of factors. The case of Trieste, the surprising single case of a settled conflict among members of opposing blocs, has also to be explained further. The conflict became susceptible to settlement after Tito broke with the Eastern bloc. The US and Great Britain mediated an agreement between Italy and Yugoslavia by threatening to withdraw their troops which separated the contending parties and by offering massive economic inducements to both parties for a settlement.

TABLE IV

CONFLICT SETTLED

		Yes	No	Total n
	1) Opposing Blocs	1	0	1
ALIGNMENT	2) Same Bloc	3	5	8
	3) Member vs. unaligned	3	3	6
	4) Both unaligned	7	2	9
	Sum:	14	10	24

Source: Mandel, op. cit.

Mandel's underlying hypothesis deals more subtly with the effect of third parties on conflict de-escalation. He is interested in the likelihood of third parties getting involved in the conflict as <u>participants</u>. Thus, he focuses on the potential for increasing the scope of the conflict rather than on the effectiveness of an alliance structure (bloc) in muting conflict when compared to inter-bloc conflicts. Simple bilateral conflicts can rapidly increase in severity while more complex trilateral relations seem to prevent disputes from escalating.

> <u>This assumption is indirectly compatible with some of the previous theorizing about bipolar and multipolar systems</u>.... Although conflict may be equally or more frequent in multipolar systems, it tends to be less severe because it is diffused pluralistically among a larger number of viewpoints and cross-pressures from more interdependent actors. If three nations are mutually contiguous, then any border dispute between the two of them is difficult to isolate from the whole web of relations among the three. <u>Rather than using (as most previous studies have) common borders simply as a means of indicating chances for interaction and threat, this hypothesis is able to use them to indicate potentially interlocking interests as well</u>.[7]

By utilizing the "four-color" theorem which demonstrates that "four colors are sufficient to color any map so that no two regions with a common boundary line are colored with the same color,"[8] Mandel is able to show that no more than four nations can be mutually contiguous. From this theorem he devises four classes of sets: Class A in which a state has no neighbor (island, although this is obviously a problematic assertion by Mandel!), Class B in which two states are mutually contiguous, and Classes C and D in which three states and four states respectively are mutually contiguous. A and D are of little relevance since most states are members of B and C.

His analysis yields the following conclusions. Resource-related border disputes involved pairs of states that were members of opposing blocs. However, conflict is most likely to arise out of border disputes between two contiguous states which have disagreements relating to territorial issues. The condition most likely "to lead to an existing border dispute spreading to third parties is when two adjacent nations are members of opposing blocs."[9] It is not entirely clear what theoretical implications can be drawn from the rather surprising impact which bloc membership has in resource conflict as distinguished from ethnically induced conflict. Nevertheless, some of Mandel's findings are more interesting than the conventional and rather crude generalizations of either L.F. Richardson,[10] or Deutsch and Singer.[11] Richardson found that the number of a nation's borders is positively associated with the number of its inter-state wars. Singer and Deutsch suggested that conflict among nations in the same alliance is muted in range and intensity when compared to other bilateral conflicts. Focusing instead on the scope of conflict, Mandel's work appears to conceptualize the influence of formal and informal alignments and of third parties. This explains some of the counterintuitive findings on the ineffectiveness of hegemonic powers in "ending" or settling a dispute.[12] The importance of the hegemony lies not in settling the dispute but in limiting it and in preventing third party involvement across bloc lines. Mandel argues that a dispute between primary antagonists in opposing blocs is more likely to produce direct third party involvement than disputes in the same bloc because "within bloc disputes seem less likely to involve issues of major concern to other nations -- less likely to be proxies for bloc rivalries and within bloc disputes seem less likely to have crucial destabilizing effects on the distribution of power in the international system."[13]

For a more detailed picture it is necessary to go beyond the analysis of global patterns to which this section was devoted. The case studies are designed to explore in greater detail the historical circumstances of particular disputes. Nevertheless, before such case studies can be assessed some further conceptual clarifications are in order. It is particularly important to understand the links between a dispute and the likelihood of its escalation. This in turn suggests ways to control escalation and to resolve these conflicts in a peaceful fashion.

III

Dispute -- Conflict -- Settlement

Conflicts arising out of boundary disputes, we have seen, show a curious pattern of longevity and, in most of the cases, relatively low levels of violence. This contradicts the popular impression that boundary conflicts are pure zero-sum conflicts, and the assumption that boundary conflicts are very likely to lead to wars.

Some theoretical considerations explain why the historical record fails to support these intuitive inferences. Admittedly, boundary disputes when represented as static bargaining games appear to resemble zero-sum conflicts. In the real world, however, boundary disputes show features of mixed motive games where the contending parties have conflicting as well as common interests for the simple reason that boundaries mark not only pieces of territory but also mediate social relationships and exchanges. Even if one state has the power to impose a "settlement," such a strategy can be costly, create ill will in the future, and give rise to revanchisme. Thus, the settlement of the Iranian-Iraqi territorial dispute in the Shatt-al-Arab was short-lived and led to a major war as soon as Iraq perceived an opportunity and felt strong enough to challenge the status quo. A "settlement" is stable only if it gives rise to a new relationship between the contending parties and if expectations about normal relations can develop in the face of residual tensions and disappointments. "Wars" or violence do not end disputes. Exactly because a violent resolution is costly and frequently does not promise a mutually acceptable "normal" state of affairs afterwards, states prefer most often to avoid paying the costs either of violent confrontation or of losing "face" over their claims by, so to speak, keeping the dispute on the "back burner."

It is best therefore not to conceive of boundary conflicts as static bargaining games but as processes. In order to analyze further this process, it is useful to introduce the following stages: (1) dispute (or conflict of interest of which "competition" might be a subcategory), (2) conflict proper which may entail coercive moves, and (3) "settlement" which ends a particular sequence or "episode."

A dispute exists and the first stage is realized when the following conditions are met:

a) Two (or more) distinctive parties must exist and have contact with each other.

b) They must pursue mutually exclusive and/or mutually incompatible, scarce values.

c) This gives rise to mutually opposed actions and reactions. [14]

A dispute can exist only if both parties are aware of it. Nevertheless, it might be in the interest of one party to pretend that a "normal" state of relations rather than a dispute exists; this can be a subtle way of shifting the blame for the deterioration of relations. Some of the curious responses to our questionnaire can be interpreted in this way when, e.g., one party denies and the other insists that there is a dispute.

During the dispute stage normal relations are strained, but the striving of each party is directed towards the scarce object for which each side competes. Established rules and principles govern this competition and bind the strategic actions of the opponents. The dispute is perceived as a conflict of interests. In the case of conflict the nature of the interaction changes. The chief objective is now no longer the scarce object but rather the breaking of the will of the opponent. As Timasheff aptly remarked:

> In extreme, violent conflict...there is a temporary relegation of the original goal to a secondary position and substitution of force itself in its place. The elimination or substantial weakening of the opponent, the breaking of his resistance becomes the immediate goal. It should also be clear that in violent conflict the goal substitution is much more complete than in other forms of conflict.[15]

The conflict stage is therefore different from that of a dispute by the fact that:

(1) The actions of the actors exhibit behavior aiming at the destruction, injury, impediment or control of the other party or parties.

(2) Attempts are made to acquire power by acquiring scarce resources used to pressure the opposed party.[16]

In the conflict stages there is a process of escalation in which fewer and fewer alternatives are available and the focus of attention shifts more and more away from each states's interests to efforts at subjugating the opposing state.

This has important implications for a theory or understanding of conflict as well as for the practice of mediating conflict. "Rather than looking for the sources of conflict or its underlying causes like economic gain, honor, race, class structure or the stratification of the international system, we had better address ourselves to questions like this: under what circumstances do decision makers decide that all viable alternatives are exhausted save one -- the resort to violence."[17] As Mack and Snyder observe,

> Is it possible to identify a point of no return in a

conflict relationship progressing toward war? What effect do the nature, flow and interpretation of information have on the foreclosure of alternatives? Analyzing war decisions along these lines represents a much more fundamental approach than the listing of causes of war or attribution of single overpowering motives to nations.[18]

The focus on breaking the other's will makes it necessary then to pay particular attention to factors of power. Thus, if one antagonist's great preponderance of power is known to both, this will most probably prevent the eruption of a violent conflict. Even if the weaker party is extremely dissatisfied, "peace" ensues. Overturning the status quo is perceived as either impossible or too costly. Thus, the Japanese-Soviet boundary dispute over the Northern Islands is unlikely to escalate, and dissatisfaction with the boundary situation in Germany is unlikely to result in violent conflict. In the case of Germany, the territorial dispute has de-escalated to some minor "positional" issues. Because of the clear-cut bloc lines and the underlying balance of terror, territorial aspirations are muted. The two German states have set up joint commissions for the delineation of the boundary on the Elbe river and in the German Bay of the Baltic.

This line of reasoning accords with the empirical findings of F.S. Pearson who tried to demonstrate the existence of a relationship between forceful intervention and the respective sizes of powers locked into a border dispute.[19] He found that middle and small powers more often intervene for territorial interests than do large powers. Great powers not only hold positions that are difficult to challenge but have settled their territorial disputes in an earlier period of expansion.

Geoffrey Blainey's research concerning the causes of war, which is based on an examination of the major international conflicts since 1700, provides a theoretical rationale for such explanatory hypotheses.[20] He finds that war is likely to break out when there is a disagreement of states over their relative strength and ends when the states involved find a way of assessing through the test of arms their respective power.[21] This theory assumes that states are rational actors and make their decision on a closely calculated cost-benefit analysis, while other studies properly emphasize the irrationalities of decision-making in international life and lay stress on misperceptions or fervent nationalism of the actors involved. Nevertheless, a rational actor approach to the explanation of war can be helpful. The complexities of particular international disputes may be taken into account subsequently.

The outbreak of World War II is conventionally taken as an indication of Hitler's "irrationality," as well as of the inade-

33

quacy of a "rational" explanation of that event. Without wanting to deny the validity of any particular assessment of the "Fuehrer," we must remember that World War II was a series of wars (Poland, France, Balkans etc.) which historiography has made one historic episode;[22] several wars which were happening sequentially or simultaneously have been aggregated into one frame. This naturally does not mean that statesmen like Roosevelt did not see the sequence of wars already as one historical event. Nevertheless, Blainey points out:

> The Second World War began simply as a war between Germany and Poland on Sept. 1, 1939. As Britain and France were allies of Poland they went to war with Germany on Sept. 3; Russia invaded Eastern Poland on Sept. 14 but remained at peace with Britain and France. Thus by the end of Sept. 1939, with Poland crushed, the war had been reduced to a simple contest in which France and the British empire fought Germany with the minimum of fighting.... By the end of June 1940 Hitler had won such a triumph that his only remaining opponent was Britain and her overseas dominions. Ironically the war by the summer of 1940 was less a general war than it had been in the first month of the war.[23]

But Hitler's calculation that Britain, even when provided with some assurances for its territorial integrity, would not continue to fight proved wrong. Thus, calculations concerning the resort to violence are much more complicated than a mere look at military capabilities reveals. The decision maker has to estimate the opponent's ability to turn the capabilities into usable power when compared to his own, the opponent's resolve to project his power, and the likelihood that the antagonist will persist in fighting when the price is raised (again when compared with one's own willingness to continue). Each of these factors involves a whole host of often problematic assumptions. Thus, countries weaker in capabilities have sometimes won against considerable odds exactly because the opponent could not profit from his strength, or because the militarily weaker side has made up for its lack of capabilities by taking larger losses or because the ostensibly weaker side had greater staying power.[24] The Persian War conducted by ancient Greece is an example of the first point, while the Algeria and Vietnam conflicts illustrate the others.

In the same vein, the Falkland conflict was precipitated by a perceived lack of resolve in the adversary. Britain had shortly before withdrawn its only ship from the South Atlantic and Argentinian leaders discounted British willingness to fight. They also may have been misled by episodes in recent history which indicated that a quick fait accompli was unlikely to be reversed by the opponent's increasing the stakes.[25] Furthermore, the timing of the

Malvinas invasion clearly shows that the Argentine junta discounted British resolve if Britain did fight and believed that England would be satisfied by saving face with militarily meaningless gestures. The Argentine leaders evidently timed their invasion poorly. As Gerald Hopple writes,

> Much of the British fleet was back home for Easter when the Argentines invaded, a fact that later facilitated the very rapid assembly of a powerful British task force. If Argentina had waited for only two more months, the fleet would have been dispersed (with a group of warships as far off as the Indian Ocean). If Argentina had been willing to wait for eighteen months, its forces would have faced a Royal Navy stripped of any sea-based air power. The aircraft carriers Hermes and Invincible, the backbone of the successful British attempt to retake the islands, were slated for retirement and sale to Australia; the government had cancelled plans and contracts for any new carrier construction. Furthermore, Argentina was in the process of acquiring new arms and would have been much better equipped a few months later. [26]

Not only did the Argentinians underestimate Britain's will to fight and accept losses, they also overestimated the motivation of their own troops. National folklore had always emphasized the intensity of Argentina's grievance and had contrasted it with Britain's half-hearted interests in the Falklands.

Our discussion of the escalatory process stressed the process by which the goal of breaking the will of the other party substitutes for the goal of achieving a scarce value when a dispute (conflict of interest) is transformed into a (violent) conflict. Similarly, we can hypothesize that conflict has deescalated when the parties cease to view the breaking of the will of the other as their objective and revert to a definition of the situation in terms of conflicting interests. The bargaining process through which the parties try to arrive at a common understanding and thus at a settlement has two aspects: first and most obviously, as classical bargaining theory indicates, there is an agreement concerning the distribution of scarce values indicated by the location of the point of settlement on the possibility boundary (the line Q - T in Figure I).

While Q would be the most preferred outcome for A (and T for B) the distributional bargain concerns whether party A has enough bargaining strength to make B settle on "alpha" or whether B can, in turn make it stick on a position on the curve more favorable to it, say "beta." (Anything west of Q - T is suboptimal, anything east unrealistic.) This bargaining process can be further analyzed in terms of the sequence of positions (offer, counteroffer, etc.) the parties take. Questions of "commitment," of bluffing and threats, are then the psychological factors also to be taken into account.[27] Furthermore, in bargaining a "hard" negotiating style dominates the "soft" one. "If the hard bargainer insists on concessions and thus makes threats while the soft bargainer yields in order to avoid confrontation and insists on agreement, the negotiating game is biased in favor of the hard player."[28] Therefore, the conventional emphasis on psychological factors to threats and bluffs appears at first to be justified.

Figure I

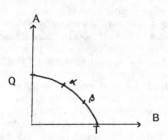

But conceptualizing negotiations and settling only in these positional terms leaves out an important <u>second</u> dimension, i.e. the definition of the game of negotiation, or <u>what has to be agreed upon before even a bargaining space</u> (represented above in the diagram) <u>can come into existence</u>. This second dimension is often ignored because classical bargaining theory does not explicitly deal with the construction of the bargaining space (unless one constructs a meta-game). We are usually not aware of this dimension because with one and the same move, we most often play the distributional <u>as well</u> as the "meta-game." As Fisher points out:

> Each move you make within a negotiation is not only a move that deals with rent, salary or other substantive questions; it also helps structure the rules of the game you are playing. Your move may serve to keep negotiations within an ongoing mode, or it may constitute a game-changing move.
>
> This second negotiation by and large escapes notice because it seems to occur without conscious decision. Only when dealing with someone from another country, particularly someone with a markedly different cultural background, are you likely to see the necessity of establishing some accepted process for the substantive negotiations. But whether consciously or not, you are negotiating procedural rules with every move you make, even if those moves appear exclusively concerned with substance.[29]

This has several important implications for bargaining and settlements. Rather than focusing on positions (which nearly always have the implications that what I win, you lose), it becomes necessary to redefine the game. The focus then turns away from positions to underlying interests and to the invention of new options rather than to the problem of distribution.

Fisher gives an excellent example of this type of bargaining which he calls "principled negotiation." During the Camp David negotiations, the positions of Egypt and Israel concerning the Sinai appeared irreconcilable. Israel wanted to keep most of the Sinai and Egypt was not satisfied with less than the restoration of Egyptian sovereignty. Attempts at drawing a compromise line, i.e. dividing the territory, failed time and time again. Only by looking at the underlying interests, instead of the distributional problem, did a solution appear. Israel's position was based on its security interest in not having Egyptian tanks near its borders, while Egypt wanted to reclaim territory that was of great symbolic significance to her. The demilitarization proposals restoring Egyptian sovereignty but demilitarizing the area made a settlement possible that no pure positional deal could have achieved. [30]

Reconciling interests rather than positions is possible because of two reasons: first, interests can usually be satisfied by more than one position. Second, behind conflicting interests there are usually shared and compatible interests so that by redefining options the "mixed motives" become clearer. Redefining the game by generating options also helps to base the settlement on some mutually agreeable and therefore "objective standard" that can be invoked if difficulties arise in the future. It thereby enhances the chance that the settlement will survive the euphoria of the moment. Especially if the settlement requires more sacrifices from one side, it is important to involve it actively in reaching that conclusion. Thus, even when conflicts are resolved in a judicial setting, a court not only declares one party a "winner" and the other a "loser" but also justifies its decision by reference to accepted values, legal reasoning and persuasive arguments. [31] If such principled reasoning is intrinsic to the acceptance of a decision in cases when the parties have already accepted the "authority" of a "judge," it is all the more important in bilateral negotiations where no such prior agreement exists.

Emphasizing interests and new options as well as principles also helps states to focus on the development of future relations after the settlement, rather than on the "causes" or the particular grievances that originally created the dispute. Looking backward at causes "treats our behavior as determined by prior events."[32] Looking forward at the future, however, emphasizes (shared) purposes and the potentialities awaiting realization; this breaks the stronghold of the past and sets states free to determine anew the bases of their relationships.

The great postwar European boundary disputes which were successfully settled all exhibit this essential redefinition of the game. The French - German settlement of the Saar issue was part and parcel of a comprehensive reorientation in Franco-German relations. Having agreed to a plebiscite on the Saar statute, France accepted not only German interests as legitimate, but the German chancellor himself could urge the people in the Saar to vote for the special statute, since it promised to resolve the century old German-French enmity. (Knowing that the majority would vote for a reintegration into Germany naturally made such a stance easy.)

The resolution of the Trieste issue depended on a similar redefinition of the game, brought about by the Allies and their promises of substantial economic aid for the future development of the region within a wider Yugoslav-Italian understanding.[33] In the calculation of interests, new options superseded insistence on historic rights; positional bargaining concerning the ultimate boundary included only symbolic alterations in order to shore up domestic support for the settlement.[34] Similarly, the South Tyrol dispute between Italy and Austria was settled amicably when Italy proved responsive to Austria's concerns for the German-speaking Tyroleans and accepted a "package" which provided for significant improvements of the regional autonomy as well as for a "calendar" of implementation (November 1969).[35]

Thus, in all three cases the settlement included not only a boundary agreement -- acceptance of either a newly drawn boundary as in the case of Trieste or rejection of a change as in the case of the Saar or reaffirmation of the existing boundary as in South Tyrol -- but also the acceptance of principles that from then on were to govern the exchanges mediated by the boundaries. This accords with our theoretical observations of the last chapter and also makes a more detailed investigation of the role of norms and of mediators necessary.

IV

Implicit and Explicit Third Parties

The discussion of the previous section showed the importance of a normative (or principled) framework for the formulation of settlements and the patterning of subsequent relations. This means that norms and rules allow antagonistic parties to take a step back and view their disagreement more objectively. Norms serve therefore as implicit third parties which influence the set of possible solutions and provide the stability and finality characteristic of a good settlement.

However, principles can be equivocal or conflicting principles can point toward different solutions so that renewed bargain-

38

ing might ensue. In that case, the parties can reach a settlement only if they can agree on what "weight" each party's consent has and what the relative costs are by settling on one rather than on the other "solution." Here, usually, an explicit third party becomes necessary. The functions of the third-party may be limited to establishing communications between the parties or, at the other extreme, they may involve authoritative third-party rule application (adjudication). Mediational efforts fall in the middle of this continuum. Thus, we can say that explicit third party involvement can occur in various modalities, depending upon the firmness of rule guidance employed by the third party in arriving at a decision and by the interested or disinterested character of its involvement. This leaves us with the following table of the role of third parties which incorporates the three variables of (a) interestedness and disinterestedness, (b) the firm/loose continuum and (c) implicit/explicit character of their involvement.

TABLE V

Type of Third Party

| | Disinterested | | Interested | |
	Implicit	Explicit	Implicit	Explicit
Loose	I. "fair," negotiated settlement (ex aequo et bono) (loose IL use)	II. mediation (principles and norms play a role but so do other factors, such as position of mediator)	III. empty set	IV. hegemonic arm-twisting
Firm	V. Acceptance of a strictly legal solution (end of controversy)	VI. Adjudication (arbitration, judicial settlement)	VII. empty set	VIII. Imposition of a solution upon the contending parties

MODE OF INVOLVEMENT

However, a few explanatory remarks concerning the different classes of disputes that emerge from this taxonomic attempt are in order. It should be obvious that cells III and VII are empty sets since an implicit-interested third party is difficult to imagine. In order to be classified as "interested" the parties and/or the observer must notice the claims a third party makes while trying to settle a dispute.

Similarly, cell V defines a class of events that, although not conceptually impossible, is nevertheless practically unlikely. It presupposes the absolute unequivocal "correctness" of a solution arrived at by strict reasoning, taking the relevant (legal) rules and principles into account. Unless one assumes that the issues involved do not actually allow for conflicting interpretations and unless the parties involved are willing to settle on the "correct" solution as soon as it has been found, the set is virtually empty. After all, it is the openness of legal systems and the ambiguity of norms, as well as their different weight in particular cases, which makes it necessary to resort to an authoritative decision by an explicit third party (the judge, arbitrator or mediator) in the first place. These cases fall into cells II and VI in Table V.

Finally Cell I is a marginal class due to the difficulties the contending parties have in bargaining situations in thinking impartially about the interests of the other party. Some interesting patterns emerge from a cursory view of the role of implicit and explicit third parties in resolving boundary disputes.

Implicit Third Parties: The Role of Norms and Principles

International legal prescriptions which serve as implicit third parties are perhaps most successful in positional boundary disputes. Rules such as choosing a mountain crest, watershed,[36] the "thalweg" of a river as a boundary, the 3, 4, or now 12-mile zone of territorial waters as well as the more technical rule for drawing straight base-lines,[37] provide negotiators with prescriptions that provide for principled negotiated outcomes.

Principles concerning title to territory (such as discovery, state succession, cession, occupation, accretion, and prescription) are helpful in establishing the criteria for settling territorial disputes. But these principles often lead to conflicting outcomes. They serve as justificatory arguments in the process of claim and counterclaim that states make upon each other and they shape settlements only when applied by third parties in a judicial context. Functional boundary disputes are most frequently in need of specific but comprehensive resource regimes codified in such multilateral treaties as the Continental Shelf Convention, the new United Nations Conference on the Law of the Sea Draft Treaty (UNCLOS III) and conventions which regulate, among other things, living marine resources. In some respects, functional disputes can overlap with positional ones since, for example, the delimitation of a fishing zone depends upon the drawing of baselines. For "historical reasons" the equidistance principle may also be modified for maritime or continental shelf boundary delimitation, establishing exclusive rights.

If these principles cause overlapping claims and/or the par-

40

ties cannot either find a way in assigning differential weight to competing principles or invent new options, explicit third party involvement becomes necessary. Similarly, for the maintenance of a regime, different types of third-party involvement may be necessary. Property rules necessitate enforcement mechanisms, management regimes for resources require effective monitoring agencies and dispute settling institutions, and finally, newly-emerging problems arising out of the interdependencies created by different functional activities may make continuous institutional adjustment (law creation) necessary, either interstitially through "cases" in courts or through lawmaking conventions. But these third-party roles are rather different from the more narrow focus of third-party involvement in settling a conflict which must concentrate on changing the preoccupation of the parties in breaking each other's will and on creating a more constructive adjustment of interests.

Explicit Third Parties

On the most formal side, where the explicit party uses pre-existing rules and principles in order to "decide" the dispute, the settlement has an expressly judicial character. A short review of different types of judicial activity, i.e. adjudication and arbitration, shows these to play a modest rule with arbitration predominating over adjudication. Arbitration offers a much higher degree of control over the proceedings by the parties involved. Through the specification of applicable rules, the provisions for the conduct of the proceedings in the compromis and the freedom of selecting the arbitrators, the parties retain a good deal of influence on the outcome. This retention of control includes the possibility of declaring the award null and void[38] if it can be shown that the decision is based on reasons and principles other than those specified (excès de pouvoir).

Some of the more recent arbitrations concerned the border dispute between Chile and Argentina (1966), the Beagle Channel dispute which was settled by the Pope (1984), the Rann of Kutch dispute between Pakistan and India (1968), and the Lake Lanoux dispute between Spain and France (1957). Decisions redefining the issues and making awards on the basis of considerations ex aequo et bono have been extremely rare in both types of proceedings. The arbitration settling the Chaco war is sometimes cited as a case of ex aequo et bono resolution but such an interpretation is doubtful since the award did little more than ratify the existing military stalemate. On the other hand, equitable principles have sometimes been invoked in a decision. The Rann of Kutch arbitration awarded two deep water inlets to Pakistan on these grounds, and in the North Sea Continental Shelf case, the final determination of boundaries was based on equitable considerations.

Direct judicial settlements of boundary disputes have been rare. Since 1945, the ICJ has been active in the settlement of four land boundary disputes: the Minquier and Ecrehos Islands (1953), the Frontier Land Case between Belgium and the Netherlands (1959), the dispute between Honduras and Nicaragua (1960) and the Temple of Preah Vihar case between Thailand and Cambodia (1962). The maritime boundary between Guinea-Bissau and Guinea was delimited in February 1985. The land boundary dispute between Burkina Faso (Upper Volta) and Mali is still under its consideration. Five other cases involved continental shelf boundaries: the North Sea Continental Shelf case (1969), the Anglo-French case (1977), the Tunisian-Libyan Continental Shelf demarcation (1982), the issue concerning the boundaries in the Gulf of Maine between the US and Canada (1984) and the Libyan-Maltese Continental Shelf delimitation (1985).

Mediation efforts by individual states and international organizations have been numerous. In this respect the US mediation leading to the Camp David accords and the Soviet mediation in Tashkent in 1966 of the Pakistani-Indian conflict over Kashmir are the most salient examples. The OAS was active twice in the Honduran-Nicaraguan dispute (1957 and 1961) and finally persuaded both parties to submit to judicial settlement. The OAS also attempted to mediate the Rio Lauca (1962) dispute between Chile and Bolivia but without success. The Organization of African Unity was similarly unsuccessful in its effort to make its influence felt in the Algeria-Morocco dispute (1963-64) by creating a peace keeping force in a neutralized border zone. The Association of South East Asian Nations (ASEAN) was apparently instrumental in bringing about Philippine abandonment of a claim to parts of Sabah. To show its good will, the Philippines dropped its demands at a 1977 ASEAN meeting.

UN activities have been largely concerned with the defusing of military conflicts through "preventive" diplomacy. Since the Palestinian problem is not really a boundary problem, no further comment on the importance of UN peace keeping in the Middle East is necessary. Nevertheless, in a few instances a UN presence provided some valuable services. Although UN troops were not very successful in supervising a mutual withdrawal in the Kashmir conflict until the Soviet mediation occurred, they nevertheless prevented further escalation by keeping the cease-fire alive. In 1962-63 the UN administered West New Guinea for seven months in order to effect the transition from the Netherlands to Indonesia. Although this was not a case of a mediation effort, it nevertheless was an important part of implementation of the Indonesian-Dutch agreement. Most recently Venezuela and Guyana have asked the Secretary General for mediation efforts[39] in their long-standing boundary dispute. The arbitration of that dispute in 1899 Venezuela now claims is invalid due to the corruption of the chief arbitrator.

V

Conclusion

This chapter has dealt with the conflict and settlement potential of boundary and border disputes. It showed that such disputes exhibit certain distinct patterns, e.g., that they are usually of long duration and characterized by a low level of violence. This somewhat surprising finding was explained by the fact
that boundaries not only mark off territories but also mediate
social exchanges. Disputes about boundaries are not the typical
zero-sum conflicts as may appear when the position of the separating line is treated as the most decisive feature. The expectation
of future exchanges influences bargaining even in these cases with
no readily recognizable common interests.

A focus on social relationships led then to a clearer concep-
tualization of the escalation and de-ecalation process of disputes
as well as to an appreciation of "principled" bargaining as a pro-
mising strategy. The acceptance of common norms intrinsic to principled bargaining also made necessary a closer look at the function of norms as "implicit" third parties. A theoretical and historical discussion of the role of explicit third parties followed.

The last theoretical point concerns the functional thesis
that through an unbundling of exclusive territorial rights and the
creation of functional regimes conflicts could be managed better
and peace could be achieved "in parts." An examination of the Antarctica regime leads to more cautious conclusions, although the
record is impressive up to the present. Since the logic of functional regimes depends upon the willingness of all participants to
keep the issue area "depoliticized," it can quickly come under
pressure when the conditions change on which this "logic" depends.
Thus, the success of the Antarctic regime appears to have resulted largely from the satisfaction of the superpowers with the treaty, from the marginal strategic importance of the area, from an
uneasy truce between claimant and nonclaimant states papered over
by the ambiguous language of the treaty, and from the acquiescence
of the rest of the world in the privileged status of the Consultative Members (see the Arctic-Antarctic study). Even if we assume
that the strategic consensus of the two superpowers will persist,
the ability to continue in the same way may depend in the end upon
the superpowers' ability to exclude others from decisionmaking.
One way they may do this is to advance territorial claims and defeat the idea of a common heritage once and for all. The placement
of new Soviet stations, therefore, needs to be motivated by neither a dissatisfaction with the present regime nor the Soviet
Union's determination to change the status quo. But even if such
steps are the result of a cautious policy of keeping options open,
it might challenge the vitality and survival of the present regime.

On the other hand, if the negotiation of a minerals regime results in its widespread acceptance, an important test of the Antarctic framework would have been passed. How much China's (and India's) interest in Antarctica will serve to head off some Third World criticisms will also be important.

In case no satisfactory solution to the co-administration issue can be reached, the issue of the continental shelf and of the exploitation of the deep sea under the International Seabed Authority (ISA) (assuming the UNCLOS III Draft Convention enters into force) will lead to new strains which will feed back into the unresolved issues among the claimant states. The sensitivities in this issue area were clearly demonstrated in the conflict between Argentina and the United Kingdom in February of 1976 when the British research ship Shackleton commenced exploratory investigation on the continental shelves of the Georgias and was fired upon by the Argentine ship Almirante Storni.[40] This is all the more worrisome since in spite of the presently satisfactory performance of the regime, the mechanism for dispute settlement is very weak and the escalation of conflicts therefore very likely.

Drawing some lessons from these observations is not difficult, but it is somewhat disheartening. Functional regimes and the unbundling of rights have often been advocated as solutions to the "all or nothing" concept of national sovereignty. Even if such arrangements have considerably contributed to the de-escalation of conflict, they do not resolve all issues. As the proliferation of functional regimes in Antarctica shows, such regimes need considerable cooperation from the parties involved, as well as adequate institutionalization for managing the regime and for settling disputes which arise out of it. The advantage of the "all or nothing" view of territorial sovereignty is not only its simplicity but its implicit presumption that in the face of newly-emerging problems the territorial unit (and only the territorial "sovereign") has the right to regulate matters.

If the organization of international life, however, is seen only from the perspective of the simple idea of territorial sovereignty, other equally important concerns are neglected: the equitable sharing of and access to resources, as well as the problems connected with the "tragedy of the commons" (see e.g., transnational pollution problems). The design and administration of effective regimes which serve to keep conflicts from coming to a head and to lead them towards resolution rather than escalation remains a challenging task which is in constant need of adjustment and institutionalization.

NOTES

1   Surya P. Sharma, International Boundary Disputes and International Law (Bombay, India: Tripathi, 1976), p. 2.
2   These numbers are derived from a survey largely conducted in the summer 1984 among all UN members.
3   1962 ICJ, pp. 6-146, at p. 34.
4   R.L. Butterworth, Managing Interstate Conflict 1945-74: Data With Synopses (Pittsburgh: University of Pittsburgh, Center of International Studies, 1976).
5   Robert Mandel, "Roots of the Modern Interstate Border Dispute," Journal of Conflict Resolution, vol. 24 (1980), pp. 427-54, at p. 425.
6   Ibid., p. 451.
7   Ibid., p. 439.
8   T. Saaty and P. Kainen, The Four-Color Problem, Assaults and Conquests (New York: McGraw Hill, 1977), p. 4.
9   Mandel, "Roots of the Modern Interstate Border Dispute," op. cit., p. 450.
10 L.F. Richardson, Statistics of Deadly Quarrels (Pittsburgh: Boxwood, 1960).
11 K.W. Deutsch, and J.D. Singer, "Multipolar Power Systems and International Stability," World Politics, vol. 16 (1964), pp. 390-406.
12 See, the discussion above about bloc membership and conflict resolution in boundary disputes.
13 Mandel, "Roots of the Modern Interstate Border Dispute," op. cit., p. 456.
14 Friedrich Kratochwil, International Order and Foreign Policy (Boulder: Westview, 1978), p. 33. Also see, Raymond Mack and Richard Snyder, "The Analysis of Conflict -- Toward an Overview," in Claggett Smith, ed., Conflict Resolution: Contributions of the Behavioral Sciences (Notre Dame, Ind.: University of Notre Dame Press, 1971).
15 Nicholas Timasheff, War and Revolution (New York: Sheed and Ward, 1965), p. 63.
16 Kratochwil, International Order and Foreign Policy, op. cit., p. 33.
17 Ibid., p. 31.
18 Mack and Snyder, "The Analysis of Conflict," op. cit., p. 13.
19 F.S. Pearson, "Geographical Proximity and Foreign Military Intervention," Journal of Conflict Resolution, vol. 18 (1974), pp. 432-460.
20 Geoffery Blainey, The Causes of War (New York: McMillan, 1973).
21 Ibid., especially Ch. 16.
22 The same is probably true of most "hegemonic" wars which alter the international pecking order. Thus, Thucydides' Peloponnesian War is a creation of his historiography linking two periods of conflict between Sparta and Athens and the

Sicilian Expedition into "one" historical "event."

23 Blainey, The Causes of War, op. cit., p. 237.

24 For a fundamental discussion of the problematique of the power of nations see Klaus Knorr, The Power of Nations (New York: Basic Books, 1975). For the problems of why and how a weaker state can win wars by accepting greater losses see Steven Rosen, "A Model of War and Alliance," in Julian Friedman, Christopher Bladen, and Steven Rosen, eds., Alliance in International Politics (Boston: Allyn and Bacon, 1970), pp. 217-237.

25 The British withdrew of the ice patrol ship Endurance in June 1981 in spite of the warnings of the British Foreign Office that this might be a signal that could be misread in Buenos Aires. For a further discussion see Lawrence Freedman, "The War of the Falkland Islands, 1982," Foreign Affairs, vol. 61 (Fall 1982), pp. 196-210. The Argentine calculation was apparently based on the following facts. Iran had successfully seized several islands at the mouth of the Persian Gulf, China had occupied the Paracels, Vietnam seized the Spratleys, Indonesia had taken over East Timor, and Turkey invaded Cyprus, establishing a separate state. While protests accompanied all of these occupations, none of the outcomes was reversed.

26 Gerald Hopple, "Intelligence and Warning, Implications and Lessons of the Falkland Islands War," World Politics, vol. 36 (1984), pp. 339-361, at 351-352.

27 See, e.g., Thomas Schelling, Arms and Influence (New Haven: Yale University Press, 1966).

28 Roger Fisher and William Ury, Getting to Yes (New York: Penguin, 1981), p. 9.

29 Ibid., p. 10.

30 Ibid., p. 42.

31 For the stress on the persuasive rhetorical character of many legal arguments see, Friedrich Kratochwil, "Is International Law 'Proper' Law," Archiv fuer Rechts und Sozialphilosophie, vol. 69 (1983), pp. 13-46.

32 Fisher and Ury, Getting to Yes, op. cit., p. 54.

33 John Campbell, Successful Negotiations: Trieste 1954 (Princeton: Princeton University Press, 1976).

34 This concerned some elevated ground on the outskirts of Trieste (Punta Sottile) on which Italy insisted.

35 Heinrich Siegler, Oesterreich Chronik, 1945-72 (Wien Bonn Zuerich: Siegler and Co. Verlag, 1973), pp. 52-72.

36 See Sharma, International Boundary Disputes and International Law, op. cit., for an exhaustive discussion of the applicable legal principles.

37 In a survey of 128 coastal states, of which 70 have proclaimed deviations along short and straight lines, 20 cases violated the letter and spirit of the UNCLOS draft (ICNT); 23 cases showed exact compliance. In 19 cases sufficient information was not available to make an assessment possible. In

some cases the actual delineation and the stated principles significantly diverge, and thus only partial compliance can be presumed. See J.R.V. Prescott, <u>Boundaries and Frontiers</u> (London: Croom Helm, 1978), Ch. 5.

38 Most recently Argentina (January 1978) has rejected the arbitral award of the British Queen in the Beagle Channel dispute on these grounds.

39 Letter from the Venezuelan Foreign Office to the authors.

40 Auburn, <u>Antarctic Law and Politics</u>, op. cit., p. 54-55.

PART II

Case Study 1

THE FALKLANDS/MALVINAS DISPUTE

There is as much disagreement about the history of the Falklands Islands as about their legal status. They are islands in the South Atlantic, 480 miles northwest of Cape Horn (see Map 1). Since they are well beyond any recognized territorial sea claims, they clearly constitute a territorial rather than a boundary dispute. Their discovery might well have been made by Amerigo Vespucci in April 1502, though recorded sightings start with Estaban Gomez of Magellan's expedition in 1520 for Spain, John Davis in 1592, and Richard Hawkins in 1594 for England. Argentina rejects British claims to discovery because Spanish maps record the Islands as early as 1522, while English maps of the period contain no references to the Islands.

The first settlement on the islands, both countries agree, was made by the Frenchman Louis Antoine de Bougainville in 1764. The settlement of Port Louis was ceded to the Spanish in 1767 by Louis XV, possibly to placate Spain with whom France had just lost the Seven Years' War to Britain. Port Louis was renamed Port Soledad. Independently and claiming no knowledge of the existence of the French settlement, the English established Port Egmont on West Falkland Island in 1766. Both Great Britain and Argentina acknowledge that the British colony was forced to leave in 1770. By a Spanish declaration on January 22, 1771, the British were allowed to return to the colony on the condition that the restoration not prejudice the question of sovereign ownership of the Islands. After three years the British colony was disbanded because of costs, though a plaque and flag claiming the Islands in the name of George III was left behind.

Spain withdrew its settlement at Port Soledad also because of costs in 1811, leaving behind a similar plaque and marker claiming the territory. In 1816 Argentina claimed independence from Spain. In 1820 Argentina sent a ship to claim sovereignty over the territory, and in 1823 it appointed a governor for them. Only in 1826 was an Argentine settlement reestablished under the leadership of Louis Vernet, a Frenchman chartered to help the settlement and administer the fisheries around the islands. Vernet was appointed governor of the Islands in 1829. He tried to control seal hunting near the Island's waterways and attempted to keep out alien vessels. Trespassing violations continued. On July 30, 1831 he seized an American schooner, and seized two more by the next week. The US government sent the USS Lexington to Port Soledad where it arrived

MAP 1

THE FALKLAND ISLANDS

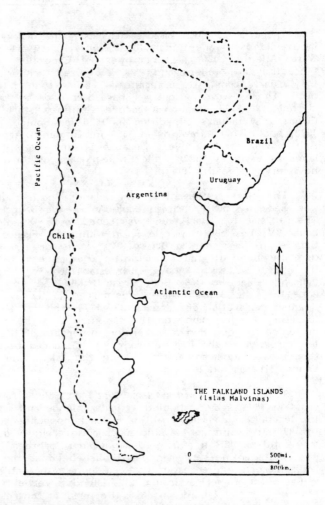

on December 28. The ship's crew deported the Argentine settlers and destroyed the Fort. The United States declared the Islands free from any government.

The English sent two warships that arrived at Port Soledad on January 1, 1833 to reclaim the Islands. Meanwhile, the Argentines had resettled the Port as a penal colony and frontier garrison. At the time the British arrived, an Argentine schooner and crew were there suppressing a revolt in the prison. Over Argentine protests the British raised the flag, and the garrison yielded peacefully and departed. Since that date the British government has seen to the Islands' administration, settlement, and defense. In 1845 it became a Crown Colony of the usual British type with a governor, legislative council, and executive council.

The Argentine Position

Argentina's claim, as it must, relies on events preceding the British takeover in 1833. It bases its claim on the purported Spanish discovery of the islands which would antedate the British claim by almost 80 years. In 1493 Pope Alexander VI awarded Spain all territories west of an imaginary line 100 leagues west of the Cape Verde Islands; the Treaty of Tordesillas between Spain and Portugal in 1494 accepted this division but specified the line at 370 leagues West of the Cape Verde Islands in between the 48th and 49th degrees of latitude. The Falklands would fall to the West of this line and be clearly Spanish. Argentina also relies on the history of treaties which Spain signed with England in which England recognized Spanish sovereignty over the islands. These treaties include the Treaty of Madrid, signed July 1670, and the Treaty of Utrecht, signed July 1713.[1] In 1790 both nations agreed to prohibit the founding of new colonies off the South American coast and preserve the status quo.[2]

For Argentina, finally, British recognition of the Spanish declaration of 1771 that allowed the re-establishment of the English settlement was an express recognition of the Spanish claim to the territory. Argentina naturally claims all the benefits of Spain's discovery and involvement with the Islands to which it succeeded when it gained independence from Spain.

Argentina claimed the Islands implicitly in its 1815 declaration of independence when, by the rule of uti possidetis, it succeeded to Spain's dependency of Rio de la Plata. The rule of uti possidetis legitimated claims to lands by Latin American states not necessarily under effective state control. Agreement on this principle removed a major source of friction among the new states because each had inherited a distinct Spanish administrative region and calmed their fear that the European colonial powers would claim land not spoken for as res nullius. Thus, while Brazil claimed its territory when it had explored only one-tenth of it,

53

Argentina claimed the Falklands, only four years later sending a ship to explore and repossess the Islands abandoned by Spain in 1811.[3]

The second argument supporting Argentina's claim to the Islands is their history of peaceful administration. Spain appointed 19 governors for the Islands from 1774 until Argentina's independence. Significantly, England recognized Argentina's independence in 1825 without making reservation to Argentina's declaration in 1820 that publicly claimed possession of the Islands. Argentine governors were administering the territory, resettled by Argentina, when Britain took control of the colony in 1833. Since that date Argentina has constantly voiced its claim to the Islands, not recognized Britain's patent, and believed that the 1833 armed usurpation was an international delict which it could rectify only by retaking the Islands -- as it did in 1982.

Additionally, Argentine authorities claim that the Islands rest on continental shelf belonging to the mainland and are therefore geographically related to Argentina. Their proximity makes them logically related to South America, not the United Kingdom. Nor can self-determination of current residents be a relevant consideration in Argentina's view. Argentina does not deny that the inhabitants have human rights, but asserts that they cannot be the deciding factor in judging the transgression of international law evidenced by Britain's armed acquisition of the Islands against legal norms.

The British Position

The United Kingdom disputes the Argentine claims on historic, legal, and ethnic grounds. Regarding the discovery of the Islands, Britain believes the Davis and Hawkins sightings are more verifiable than the Spanish claims and also points to the first known landing on the Islands by Captain John Strong in 1690. The Treaty of Tordesillas, according to the British position is not applicable to the Islands because they were discovered one hundred years after the treaty was signed and therefore could not have been promulgated with the Islands' disposition in mind.

The British argue that Spain never ceded its right of claim to the Falklands to Argentina. By granting independence to what was known at the time as the, "United Provinces of Plata," the right of sovereignty over other territories was not thereby transferred. Further, Spain abandoned the Islands in 1811 and the area reverted to terra nullius before Argentina acceded to Spain's possessions. The attempt of Buenos Aires to reclaim the territory in 1820 and resettle it in 1826 was privately undertaken and unsuccessful.[4] The Argentine effort to defend its claim against alien fishing vessels was unsuccessful and, yielding to the USS Lexington, settlement was disbanded without protest. In short, the Ar-

54

gentine claim was never perfected because it failed to practice effective control over the Islands.

The British eviction of the resettlers in Port Soledad in 1833 additionally weakens the Argentine claim to adequate administration and authority over the Islands. The Spanish claim to the territory may have been perfected by the expulsion and later readmission of the British by a special signed protocol in 1770-1771, but the Spanish claim lapsed with their departure in 1811 and the lack of express succession to Spain's claim at the time of independence followed by four more years of silence on the issue constitute legal abandonment.

Argentina, in Britain's view, therefore first claimed the Islands in 1820 and never practiced effective control. Therefore, British repossession of the Islands and its continuous, effective administration and protection of them since 1833 constitutes a prima facie claim to possession in international law. All arrangement for trade and supply as well as governance tie the Islands to the UK.

Additionally, all disputants recognize that the inhabitants of the Falklands are British in ethnic origin, tied by language, religion, and family to England. This is the basis for the the third and preeminent claim of Britain to the Falklands, that the right of self-determination of all colonized territories should be applied to the Falklands. The British claim they have pursued this goal with good faith in their other colonial territories and that they intend to apply that norm of international law as expressed in Article 73 of the UN Charter to the Falklands. Representatives elected by the semi-autonomous Islands government have consistently favored close links with the UK, as have all the plebiscites of the population. Therefore, continued British possession of the Islands is not merely legal, but mandated by the spirit of the UN Charter and prevailing legal norms.

While the Argentine claim is weakened by the lack of clear cession of the territory by Spain to Argentina and the unperfected claim in its own right to administration over the Islands, the British position is also flawed. The British claim to administrative competence is weakened by Britain's decision to relinquish postal service and fuel supplies for the Falklands to Argentine management in the decade before the war of 1982.[5] The Islands are also dependent on the mainland for major medical care and education -- the latter admittedly to British schools operating in Argentina.

More significantly, it is doubtful whether the principle of self-determination can be applied in this context. The norm derived from the need to correct the injustices done under colonization of inhabited lands over the past two centuries is of uncertain applicability to the peopling of empty lands to solidify influence. "International practice applies the principle of self-determination to 'colonial enclaves' only in very limited circumstances" and, while Gibraltar may fit such circumstances, the Falklands are a less likely candidate.[6] The UN General Assembly has classified the Falklands as non-self-governing, but the Assembly has not considered them appropriate for self-determination and independence. The Falklands are, however, well administered in compliance with the spirit and letter of Article 73 of the Charter and Resolution 66 (I). The British settlers constitute not an indigenous population whose past rights may be in need of redress but "a settler population who replaced the legitimate previous Argentine inhabitants."[7] On the other hand, one might argue that Argentine settlement of the Islands, if not defendable by Argentina, was not legally founded.

Analysis

Both sides have strong and weak points in their respective cases. The dispute is essentially a conflict of rights: what Britain sees as the right of self-determination conflicts with Argentina's view of the right of a state to territorial integrity. What Britain considers a concerns for the rights of persons, Argentina sees as a question of the rights of states, and both sets of rights can be supported by principles of international law. Argentina perceives its right to pursue decolonization of the Islands in its geopolitical interest as undeniable. Britain believes the structure of law legitimates its claims to territories it effectively possesses, administers, and controls. (The British have been in the Falklands longer than the Americans have been in California.)

Negotiations to resolve the conflict were hindered by different perceptions of the problem. In 1946 the UK reportedly listed the Islands as a territory that would ultimately be granted autonomy, but the British government did not agree to talks on the issue until 1966. UN Resolution 2065 (XX) was the basis of Britain's acceptance of negotiations and this resolution significantly includes both the objectives of UN Resolution 1514 (XV) on colonial independence and "the interests of the population of the Falkland Islands." This phrasing however could not gloss over the differing Argentine and British perceptions of the situation.

Argentine expectations escalated when negotiations began, but the meager results were disillusioning.[8] As alternatives were discarded, Argentina became more discouraged about settling the dispute peacefully. In August 1968 the two countries agreed to a Memorandum of Understanding which generally noted that if the UK were satisfied with the guarantees and safeguards of Argentina for the Islanders' rights, Britain would recognize Argentine sovereignty over the Islands.[9] Subsequently the UK rejected the Memorandum as a public statement of intent, mostly for domestic political reasons. Nonetheless, in 1971 Britain contracted with Argentina for fuel and postal contacts with the Islands supplied from the mainland and Argentina may have in part relied on the 1968 Memorandum as evidence of a change in the British position.

The stagnation of negotiations was recognized by 1973 UN Resolution 3160 (XXVIII) and the 1976 Resolution 31/49 of the General Assembly that called for continued talks on the issue. As alternatives were discarded during negotiations, the dispute appeared less and less likely to be quickly resolved. In this context, the situation developed toward a "trigger moment" to precipitate armed conflict.

From this case study several conclusions can be drawn. A third party frequently can perform the function of creating and presenting alternative proposals for resolution. A lack of alternatives to explore gives the parties reason to believe armed conflict is the only avenue available to move the dispute toward settlement. Second, such alternatives should clarify what is really at issue between the parties. While a conflict of rights or interests may not be avoided this way, the parties will at least not be talking past each other. Armed conflict results not only when one party fails to recognize that a grievance exists -- as in the Ethiopian-Somali dispute -- but also when optimism for the acknowledged dispute's resolution is consistently frustrated.

A third conclusion follows from this case. When a conflict refines itself into two opposing legal sides, both of which can be supported by international law, there are two peaceful alternatives for resolution:(1) submission to a decision on legal grounds through adjudication, arbitration or judicial settlement in the ICJ or (2) extralegal conciliation based on equitable principles to resolve the issue with both states' interests in mind. The fact that the two sides could not agree to seek a resolution of their dispute about the Falklands along a judicial route indicates uncertainty on the part of both as to which would win in judicial fora. The non-judicial path, therefore, was taken. In the UN, Argentina had a forum it could rely on to call for decolonization of the territory and assumption of Argentine sovereignty. In the bilateral discussions, Britain was less restricted by the legalistic constraints of The Hague and the politicized forum of the UN. In the Latin approach, negotiation characterized by appreciation of formal principle, the grand idea, and national honor[10] is preferred as the basis for bargaining, but Latin negotiators do not want to be bound by the legalistic specificity and detail to which a state commits itself in legal proceedings. Britain, for the sake of pragmatic compromise, may also prefer extralegal fora. Thus, the two states prefer the same mechanism, bilateral negotiation, but for different reasons and on the basis of different sets of principles by which to resolve the dispute. Accordingly, third parties would probably be most effective if they could help to create a single set of principles to guide negotiation rather than to seek to bind the parties to legal methods of resolution.

NOTES

1   Both treaties are reprinted in Raphael Perl, The Falklands Islands Dispute in International Law and Politics (London: Oceana Publications, 1983), pp. 133-143.
2   Malvinas Islands Statement by the Representative of Argentina H.E. Dr. Jose Maria Ruda, before the Subcommittee III of the Special Committee on the Situation with Regard to the Implementation of the Declaration on the Granting of Independence to Colonial Countries and Peoples. (New York, UN, Sept. 9. 1964) in Perl, op. cit., pp. 358-359.
3   F.M. Auburn, The Ross Dependency (The Hague: Martinus Nijhoff, 1972) pp. 15-16.
4   Statement of Sir John Thomson of the UK, 2 November 1982, UNGA (XXXVII) A/37/L.3, pp. 8-9.
5   Falklands/Malvinas, Whose Crisis? (London: Latin American Bureau, 1982), pp. 3-5.
6   Perl, op. cit., p. 38.
7   General Assembly Resolution, 2065 (XX) UNGAOR 1398 (1965), p. 9.
8   Ruben de Hoyos, "Islas Malvinas or Falkland Islands: The Negotiation of a Conflict, 1945-1982," in Michael A. Morris and Victor Millan, eds., Controlling Latin American Conflicts (Boulder, Colorado: Westview, 1983), pp. 192-193.
9   A/37/553 Circulated letter of Carlos Manuel Muniz, Permanent Representative of Argentina, with Annex. 20 October 1982, pp. 7,8.
10 Glen Fisher, International Negotiation: A Crosscultural Perspective, (Chicago: Intercultural Press, 1980).

Case Study 2

ETHIOPIAN-SOMALI DISPUTE

The Ethiopian-Somali conflict is a dispute over the Ogaden region of Ethiopia that is populated by Somali tribes (see Map 2). The animosity between the two states far antedates their recent formation as sovereign nations and originates in their history as rival cultures. Coptic Christianity gained preeminence in Ethiopia by spreading its control from the Tigre and Wello regions to the Amharic seat of power in Shoah. Its sway, however, was threatened by the growth of Islam among the Somali tribes who lived on the coastline of the Horn of Africa and were easily accessible to Moslem missionaries. The first recorded battle of the Christian-Islamic competition was 1531-42 when Ahmed Gran, a Somali Islamic leader, conducted armed campaigns against Ethiopia and made deep inroads in their territory.

Since that period the history of the Horn of Africa has been one of continuous struggle between the two groups. Ethiopia had a tradition of centralized governance and leadership which over the years has helped it exert its power more effectively; in Somalia authority is shared and its culture that recognizes clan groups, clans, tribes and lineages makes it more difficult to deploy its power. This difference is reflected in the geography of the countries. Ethiopia is centered on a plateau above the Great Rift Valley which extends from the Horn down through all of East Africa. The highland plateau is more verdant, more intensively farmed and more densely populated. Somalia includes the semi-arid, sparsely-populated, low plains from the Awash river bordering the Shoa region in the West to the Indian Ocean in the East.

The border between the two states has been historically uncertain. Somalis inhabit the valley below the Ethiopian highlands and have long been subject to its strong political influence. The recent history of the border conflict starts with King Menelik II of Ethiopia. He united the highland regions under his strong leadership and, in 1887, joined with Italy in the Treaty of Uccielli which gave Italy protectorate rights over Ethiopia. The Somali clans south of Djibouti and along the coast feared the growing Ethiopian strength and potential for expansion and individually signed treaties with Great Britain for protection during the years 1884-1886. The British faced problems with their administration of the Sudan and Egypt however, and spent little effort defending the Somali region. In 1887 the Islamic city of Harar fell to Menelik and by 1891 he claimed the entire Ogaden region as part of Harar.

MAP 2

SOMALIA AND THE HORN OF AFRICA

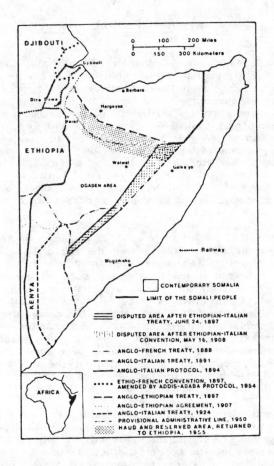

Source: John Drysdale, The Somali Dispute (New York: Praeger, 1964); reprinted by permission of Phaidon Press.

The Italians encouraged Menelik in his ambitions, but the British only used diplomatic maneuvers to defend the Somali regions. Britain's main interest was in the few port cities on the Gulf of Aden and the Indian Ocean that the country offered rather than the barren land of Somalia's interior.

In 1897, Mr. Runnel Rodd negotiated for England an agreement with Menelik that Rodd believed defined British territory and did not recognize a legal cession of the Haud region. In the compromise, Britain abandoned its claim to 67,000 miles of land in and north of the Haud, but did not formally cede it or recognize Ethiopia as the owner; Ethiopia in turn recognized British rule up to a line 50 miles west of the Harghessa. Britain effectively gave up its protection of the Somali clans' pastoral land claims but believed the treaty assured Somali rights to free use of wells and cattle grazing land on both sides of the border.[1]

Menelik read the agreement differently, however, and the border continued to be uncertain. A guerrilla war began around this time which lasted until around 1920, led by Sayyid Muhammad. Although Sayyid gained little ground for the Somalis, he became the first truly national agitator for independence because he appealed for support in his efforts not just to his own patrilineal clan but to all Somalis.

In 1908 the Italian, British, and Ethiopian governments loosely arranged a border parallel to the coastline and 180 miles inland, running from the intersection of British and Italian Somalilands south to British Kenya. This line was unchanged until 1935 when Italy attacked Ethiopia under Mussolini and took over all the Ethiopian territory. Even after British forces defeated the Italian East African Empire and Haile Selassie was reinstalled as emperor, the border has remained, although the Somali territories have passed from colonial possessions to U.N. trust territories to independent nations.

The Ethiopian Position

To Ethiopia the Ogaden is an inheritance from Italy. Ethiopia appeals to its historic relations with the Sultanates along the Gulf of Aden now inhabited by Somalis; they were internally autonomous but always tendered allegiance to the Ethiopian crown.[2] Ethiopian sovereigns maintained law and order in the Somali regions and asserted their sovereignty. During the colonial period, Ethiopia lost the northern province of Eritrea and like Somalia was a victim of the expansionism of Europe's imperial states. In 1894 France recognized an Italian sphere of influence extending to Harar including almost all of the Ogaden and the Medjertine coast.[3] That Protocol itself defined British Somaliland as the region along the North coast of the Horn with the city of Harar and its region lying on the Italian side of the boundary. A treaty

61

on May 16, 1908 drew a border between Ethiopia and Italy with the understanding that all territory up to the Italian dependency of Somaliland, all of the Ogaden and the tribes crossing it were the dependency of Abyssinia.

The present Ethiopian government sees itself as the legal successor to the regime of Haile Selassie who came to power in 1930 after the death of the Queen Regent who inherited Menelik's empire. Ethiopia views Somalia's contention that Ethiopia does not rightfully possess the area as illegal because both Ethiopia and Somalia are signatories of the Charter of the Organization of African Unity which declares "respect for the sovereignty and territorial integrity of each state" as a founding principle. (Charter of the OAU, Art. III, Para. 3) This declaration was amplified by an early OAU resolution (AHG/Res. 16[I]) stating, inter alia, that all states undertake to respect borders existing at the time of their accession to independence. (Annex to Letter from Permanent Republic of Ethiopia to the UN, 3/IX/1980, A/35/427). Further Ethiopia views the Somali encouragement of and aid for the Ogaden separatists as unlawful and against Somalia's OAU obligations to give "unreserved condemnation, in all its forms,...(to) political assassination as well as...(to) subversive activities on the part of the neighboring states." (Charter, Art. III, Para. 5) Furthermore, Ethiopia views help to Ogaden as a violation of its agreement not to create dissension in other states by fomenting or supporting racial, religious, linguistic, ethnic or other differences. (AHG/ Res. 27[II]) In fact, Ethiopia denies that a territorial dispute exists at all. It sees the problem with Somalia as a boundary delineation dispute which can be resolved by means specified under the 1908 agreement with Italy.[4] Ethiopia thus sees itself as justified in defending the Ogaden region, although it is ready to implement the Good Offices Committee recommendations made at Lagos, August 18-20, 1980, for peaceful resolution by negotiation, mediation, and conciliation or arbitration.

The Somali Position

The Somali government, like the Ethiopian, believes international law substantiates its claim to the Ogaden region. Rather than appealing to traditional principles regarding the succession of states and treaty obligations, however, they appeal to more recent though widely accepted international norms of ethnic self-determination and de-colonization.

Historically, Somalia can point to a long recorded history of ethnic Somalis living in the Harar and Ogaden regions. The ethnic Somalis claim to be the "black Berbers" of Greek history. They adopted Islam early due to the easy access of the Somali coastal plain to Arab influence from the Arabian Peninsula across the Gulf of Aden. By the 1400s the city of Harar had become a center of Islamic learning and culture. During the 15th century, however,

pressure on the Haud region (within which Harar is located) increased as Abyssinian raiding parties came down from the highlands. In reaction Ahmed Gran secured the region. Thus what Ethiopia perceives as historic "aggression" Somalia views as justified
ethnic defense.

The base-line Somalia prefers for debating the Ogaden question is the 1850s. The writings of Sir Richard Burton from pre-
colonial times note the distribution of different ethnicities in
the Horn. Significantly, the region from Harar to the northern and
eastern coasts is not identified as Abyssinian. After that point,
the history previously mentioned picks up with one notable exception: Ethiopia, united into the Abbyssinian Empire by Menelik II,
is in the Somali view just as much a party to the colonial dismem-
berment of Somalia as Italy, Britain, and France. The British protectorate failed to keep Somali autonomy and yielded Harar and the
Ogaden in treaties to Ethiopia and Italy. Britain then drew a
provisional border which has remained due to historical circumstances.

For the Somalis, colonial treaties among imperialist powers
of either European or African origin are contrary to the letter
and spirit of both the United Nations and OAU Charters. The UN
Charter sections guiding the administration of trust territories
declares the need, "to ensure, with due respect for the culture of
the people concerned, their political, economic, and educational
advancement,...(and) to develop self-government, to take due account of the political aspirations of the people...." (Charter,
Art. 73, Para. a, b) The plan of decolonialization and self-determination was not carried out by the mere establishment of independence in the two countries within their old colonial boundaries.
Thus, Ethiopia's subjugation of Somali rights of self-determination in the Ogaden vitiates principles of the UN Charter.[5]

Somalia has consistently voiced its reservation to all international statements recognizing expressly or implicitly Ethiopia's
possession of the territory and does not recognize the existence
of any border between the two states that merits demarcation. It
has brought the matter before the UN and OAU in attempts to
achieve a peaceful solution. The section of the OAU charter (Art.
III) which pledges all states to reaffirm and respect each other's
boundaries at the time of independence was specifically stated to
exclude the Somali-Ethiopian border issue.[6] The Ethiopian Prime
Minister present at the Cairo meeting in 1964 acknowledged this.
However, he referred to Para. 4 of the same Article which pledges
peaceful settlement of disputes.

The Somali-Ethiopian dispute exemplifies a situation where
territorial and boundary issues are intertwined. If a decision
could be made giving the Haud region to one country or the other,
the problem would be relatively simple. But the criteria for giv-

ing jurisdiction and deciding the issue cannot be agreed upon. At the same time, both states have very different perceptions of the history and documentary legacy of the territory. They do not share agreement on a common understanding of the underlying facts sufficient to implement common principles if they were found.

Analysis

The Somali-Ethiopian dispute is one of territory more than boundary delineation. Characteristics of the territory are critical in the two parties' perceptions of reality and the origin of the dispute in the distant past gives ample room for each side to find historic justification for its position. Ultimately, the parties disagree about whether a dispute even exists: one of the two parties, presently Somalia, will be dissatisfied with any delineation offered because of their obviously incompatible demands. Both states share a zero-sum view of the situation. Unless some new element is added or a shared principle for allocating territory, the stalemate will continue.

The Somali-Ethiopian boundary serves a significantly different function than other interstate boundaries. It serves to separate two ethnically distinct peoples, to distance them rather than serve as an interface for communication and contact. Unlike other cases (e.g., Ecuador and Peru), the dispute concerns the division of peoples more than the division of land, the organization of the polity rather than the organization of resources. This affects the political legitimacy of the state and precipitates more intransigence than is found in resource allocation situations. The boundary's social function is to create nations, not just delineate jurisdiction. The colonial legacy has aggravated but not substantially altered the problem.

NOTES

1   Tom Farer, War Clouds on the Horn of Africa (New York: Carnegie Endowment, 1976), pp. 57-58.
2   Robert F. Gorman, Political Conflict on the Horn of Africa (New York: Praeger, 1981), p. 13.
3   Annex to the British-Italian Boundary Protocol, May 5, 1894, in E. Hertslet, The Map of Africa by Treaty, Vols. I and II (London: Frank Cass, 1967), pp. 669-670.
4   Background Information on the Ethio-Somalia Problem, Mission of Ethiopia to the UN 31/VIII/1977, p. 11.
5   Go From My Country (Mogadishu: Ministry of Foreign Affairs of the Somali Democratic Republic, 1978), p. 40.
6   Record of the Cairo meeting, OAU, July 1964., cited in Go From My Country, op. cit., pp. 39-40.

Case Study 3

THE JAPANESE-SOVIET TERRITORIAL DISPUTE:
The "Northern Territories"

The dispute over what Japan calls the "Northern Territories" evolves from geography as well as inaccurate treaty references to that geography. The four disputed territories consist of islands lying off the northeast coast of Hokkaido, the principal northernmost island of the Japanese archipelago: Etorofu, Kinoshira, Shikotan and the Habomai Islands group (see Map 3). Their area totals 4,996 sq. km. and the closest is situated only 3.7 km. from Hokkaido itself.

Sakhalin, the Kuriles and the Northern Territories all form part of the Asian island chain stretching from the Kamchatka Peninsula to Formosa off the Chinese mainland. They were first known and inhabited by Japanese, but the expansion of Czarist Russia eastward in the 19th century led to contact between the Japanese and Russian peoples. In 1855 the two countries signed a Treaty of Commerce, Navigation and Delineation. This established a boundary between the islands of Uruppu and Etorofu, the islands from Uruppu north along the Kuriles being Russian and those from Etorofu south being Japanese; Sakhalin was to remain for mixed settlement. The 1875 Treaty for the Exchange of Sakhalin for the Kurile Islands designated by name and allocated to Japan the eighteen islands of the Kuriles for which Japanese sovereignty over Sakhalin was exchanged. The Treaty of Portsmouth that ended the Russo–Japanese War of 1905 gave Japan the southern half of Sakhalin again and this distribution remained for the next forty years.

On August 9, 1945 the Soviet Union joined the Allies in the war against Japan and within one month had taken the surrender of the Kuriles, the Northern Territories and Sakhalin. In the San Francisco Peace Treaty of September 8, 1951 Japan renounced "all right, title and claim to the Kurile Islands and to Southern Sakhalin Island." Because the Soviet Union did not sign that peace treaty, a Japan-Soviet Joint Declaration in 1956 allowed for trade and the normalization of relations pending a definitive peace treaty. Since then the USSR has occupied the four disputed island territories and Japan has voiced its desire to retrieve them.

The Japanese Position

The Japanese claim to the still disputed islands rests on a close reading of the documentary history between Japan and the

MAP 3

THE NORTHERN TERRITORIES

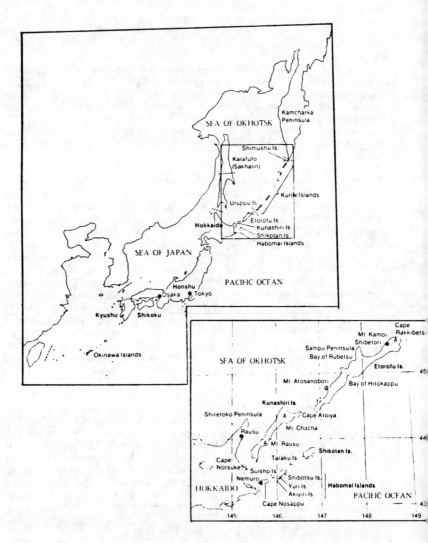

Source: <u>Japan's Northern Territories</u> (Japan: Ministry of Foreign Affairs, 1980), pp. i, 2.

Soviet Union. The Sakhalin-Kuriles Exchange Treaty of 1875 specified the Kuriles islands north of Etorofu by name. That the islands from Etorofu south were not specifically named indicates to
Japan Russia's recognition that they are inherently Japanese territory.

The Cairo Declaration of November 27, 1943 confirmed the
principles of the Atlantic Charter between the United States and
United Kingdom and declared that, at the war's conclusion, Japan
would lose all Pacific islands acquired since the beginning of
World War I in 1914. Because the Northern Territories and the
Kuriles were acquired 39 years before World War I started, the
Allied statement, in Japan's view, should have no impact upon the
issue. The Yalta Agreement of February 11, 1945 did specify that
the southern half of Sakhalin and the Kuriles were to be given to
the Soviet Union at the war's end. But the names of the Kuriles
were not specified and the Allied powers themselves later acknowledged that the Yalta agreement was "simply a statement of common
purpose by the then heads of the participating powers, and not a
final determination by those powers or of any legal effect in
transferring territories."[1] If it were to be considered a determination of the final disposition of territory, Japan may not
be bound anyway because it was not party to it and did not agree
to the terms of surrender. Furthermore, the Potsdam Declaration
(Art. 8), which presumably superseded both the Cairo and Yalta
settlements, was accepted by Japan in its capitulation and that
declaration provided for Japan's retention of the four northern
islands. At Postdam it was stated that "Japanese sovereignty shall
be limited to the islands of Honshu, Hokkaido, Kyushu, Shikoku and
such minor islands as we determine" but the declaration did not
specify the latter. In 1946 the Commander for the Allies occupying
Japan defined Japan and its adjacent islands for administrative
purposes so as to exclude the Kuriles, Habomai and Shikotan islands.[2] But the Memorandum stated "nothing in this directive
shall be construed as an indication of Allied policy relating to
the ultimate determination of the minor islands referred to in
Article 8 of the Potsdam Declaration."

The San Francisco Peace Treaty of September 8, 1951 notes
that "Japan renounces all right, title and claim to the Kurile
Islands, and to that portion of Sakhalin...over which Japan acquired sovereignty as a consequence of the Treaty of Portsmouth."
The Soviet Union, however, did not sign the peace treaty.

When the peace treaty was drafted, Japan submitted that the
Habomai, Shikotan, Kunashiri and Etorofu islands were part of Hokkaido and, unlike the Kuriles, had never belonged to any foreign
country and thus were not subject to postwar re-possession. In
1956 Japan and the USSR signed a Joint Declaration to normalize
relations. They agreed in an exchange of notes on September 29,
1956 that "negotiations for the conclusion of a peace treaty be-

tween the two countries, including the territorial issue, will continue after normal diplomatic relations have been restored between the two countries."[3] On this basis, Japan logically claims that the evidence of a dispute about the disposition of some territories was recognized by both sides. Paragraph 9 of the Joint Declaration itself notes that the USSR agreed to return the Habomai and Shikotan Islands to Japan, subject to the conclusion of a peace treaty. Therefore, in Japan's view peace treaty negotiations must still deal with the future of Etorofu and Kunashiri.

Since 1956 trade and contact betwen the two countries has increased greatly, but a peace treaty has not been concluded. In 1973 Prime Minister Tanaka visited President Brezhnev in Moscow. From statements issued at the time it appears that both sides recognized that the territorial issue still blocked agreement.

Besides this treaty history, Japan bases its claim to the islands on their early discovery and inhabitation by Japan and their distinct flora and fauna. Prior to 1945, 16,000 Japanese lived in the Northern Territories, and the fishing grounds off them had been used since ancestral times. Compared to the Kuriles, Etorofu and Kunashiri share the botanical character of Hokkaido while the Kuriles from Uruppu north are subarctic in character and akin to Kamchatka.

The Soviet Position

The Soviet perception differs greatly, though Soviet pronouncements on the dispute are sparse. The USSR does not recognize that a territorial question still exists. It finds the disposition of territories fully determined by existing international agreements and treaties.

While the Soviet Union acknowledges that the territorial questions blocked a full peace treaty in the 1950s, discussions since then have clarified that the Habomai and Shikotan Islands will be returned to Japan following the conclusion of a peace treaty. The USSR will return those islands solely as a result of negotiations; Japan remains the defeated power and must yield all land but its native islands to the World War II allies. The Yalta and Potsdam statements clearly note that the USSR is to receive the Kuriles and Sakhalin at the war's end. Further, Japanese sovereignty is to be limited to the four major islands and "such minor islands as we determine," which in the Soviet view, in no way designates the Northern Territories.

After the war, the Soviets resisted Japanese efforts to reclaim some of the Kuriles.[4] Soviet perceptions may well reflect the agreement Stalin believed he had with Roosevelt, according to which territorial transfers would take place only after a peace conference, but Soviet claims to Sakhalin and the Kuriles would be supported in return for Soviet agreement on UN trusteeship for other Japanese-conquered islands. The Soviets may have felt misled about this trade-off when the US began to support postwar Japan's claims to some of the Kuriles -- such as the Northern Territories. James F. Byrnes noted that FDR did give a promise to support Soviet claims to the islands;[5] but Soviet trust in the US, already weakened by the onset of the Cold War, declined further when a peace treaty with Japan that they were willing to sign failed to materialize. US proposals for a peace treaty in which the status of Formosa, the Pescadores, South Sakhalin, and the Kuriles would be determined by the UK, USSR, China and the US reopened questions the Soviets believed the Cairo and Yalta agreements had settled explicitly or implicitly.[6]

The Soviet Union also does not appear to acknowledge that the Northern Territories were ever thought by the Allies to be distinct from the Kuriles nor should they have been. This distinction was not referred to in wartime or postwar agreements. That the Supreme Commander for Allied Powers (SCAP) felt it advantageous to separate the Northern Territories from the main islands for governmental and administrative purposes further weakens Japan's argument about their natural contiguity with the major islands. In the San Francisco Treaty Japan specifically renounced "all right, title and claim to the Kurile Islands". The USSR, therefore, rightfully possesses the Northern Territories because of the wartime agreements so long as the Kuriles are defined as including the 'territories.' To the USSR, the final arrangement was made in the joint Soviet-Japanese declaration in which the Soviet Union stated that it will return the Habomai and Shikotan islands to Japan.

Analysis

The Japanese-Soviet dispute is a situation of two powerful developed states in contention. Their power, however, is distributed very differently. The weight of coercive force is on the Soviet side. Thus, the Soviets refuse to acknowledge that a problem exists regarding the Islands; the power imbalance allows the more powerful state to block negotiations. In the Japanese case, however, military weakness is counterbalanced by economic and industrial strength that the USSR remains anxious to tap for the development of Siberia. Implicit threats by Japan to halt Japanese cooperation in this area provides a linkage which most LDCs do not have when facing stronger powers.

The social function of the islands is also viewed differently by the two states. For the Soviet Union, possession of the Kuriles expands the defense perimeter on the one side. Japan, in turn sees possession of the Northern Territories not as a defensive matter -- it remains a state with an avowedly pacifist streak -- but as a matter of legitimacy and heritage. They are considered an ances-

69

tral land part of the Japanese people. Boundaries are to defend socialism, on the one hand, or to mark off that which is Japanese from that which is non-Japanese, on the other.

NOTES

1   Aide-Memoire to Japan from the United States, September 7, 1956. Current Documents of American Foreign Relations (Washington, D.C.: Department of State, 1959), Document 322: US position respecting Soviet-Japanese Peace negotiations.
2   Memorandum of the Supreme Commander for the Allied Powers (SCAPIN #677), January 29, 1946.
3   Cited in Japan's Northern Territories (Tokyo, Japan: Ministry of Foreign Affairs, 1980), p. 11.
4   See, e.g. Izvestia, response to Japanese Foreign Minister Yoshida's declaration of Japan's desires in a peace settlement, June 14, 1947, cited in Max Beloff, Soviet Policy in the Far East, 1944-51 (Oxford: Oxford University Press, 1953), p. 116.
5   James F. Byrnes, Speaking Frankly (New York: Harper & Bros., 1947), p. 221.
6   Beloff, Soviet Policy in the Far East, op. cit., p. 147.

Case Study 4

THE BEAGLE CHANNEL DISPUTE

As with many border problems in South America, the Beagle Channel dispute originates with the Spanish legacy of the area. In 1810 Argentina and Chile, as they gained independence from Spain, divided the Southern Cone according to the principle of uti possidetis. The area was divided on the basis of occupation, the Atlantic littoral to be Argentine and the Pacific littoral to be Chilean. In April of 1830 Captain Robert Fitzroy of the H.M.S. Beagle (with Charles Darwin aboard) discovered the channel through the archipelago connecting the two oceans at the southern tip of South America, and thus avoided the longer Strait of Magellan and the more dangerous Cape Horn route.

On July 23, 1881 Argentina and Chile signed a treaty meant to define a border in the area. Article III of the treaty stated that a vertical line at meridian 68° 34' west of Greenwich would divide the island of Tierra del Fuego into Chilean (western) and Argentine (eastern) parts. Further:

As for the islands, to the Argentine Republic shall belong Staten Island (Isla de los Estados), the small islands next to it, and the other islands there may be on the Atlantic to the east of Tierra del Fuego and off the eastern coast of Patagonia; and to Chile shall belong all the islands to the South of Beagle Channel up to Cape Horn, and those there may be to the west of Tierra del Fuego.[1]

Map 4 shows that not all islands are clearly either east and west of Tierra del Fuego, or south of the Channel. The Channel itself was not precisely defined geographically in the document and this led to the present dispute. A British arbitration in the 1898-1902 period defined the borderline in Tierra del Fuego, according to which the Straits of Magellan were placed under Chilean sovereignty. The problem of this award, however, was that it could not be implemented without infringing upon the "Oceanic Principle." The arbitration did not define the Beagle Channel geographically and only reiterated that the islands south of the Channel belong to Chile. Repeated attempts to negotiate a settlement were fruitless or resulted in agreements that were not subsequently unratified.[2] The situation continues today with an Argentine coast on the north side of the channel, a Chilean coast on the south and islands of indeterminate sovereignty in the Channel.

71

MAP 4

THE BEAGLE CHANNEL AREA

THE BEAGLE CHANNEL AREA

In 1971 a new arbitration began. It was to be conducted in accordance with the 1902 General Treaty of Arbitration between the two countries which called upon the British throne to arbitrate; the 1971 compromis provided for a panel of five judges chosen from the ICJ to act as a court of arbitration and recommend an award that the Queen could accept or deny but not change.[3] The sovereignty of the three large islands at the eastern end of the Channel -- Nueva, Picton, and Lennox -- was the main issue. To decide this, however, the Court had also to delineate what constituted the Channel itself.

The decision of May 2, 1977 did delineate a line in mid-Channel, in principle a median line which significantly utilized the northern arm of the eastern Channel mouth. It thus awarded the three islands to Chile, as they lay by its definition, south of the Channel. Argentina rejected the award as null and void on the basis of alleged inaccuracies and contradictions and it accused the court of acting ultra vires. Tension in the region increased during 1977 until the two countries signed the Act of Puerto Montt on February 20, 1978 which mandated direct negotiations to resolve the issue.

A joint negotiating commission was set up, and tension was temporarily eased while common interests in Antarctica and on economic cooperation were reaffirmed. The Channel dispute, however, was not resolved. On January 8, 1979 in Montevideo the parties agreed to Papal mediation for the purposes of guiding them in their direct negotiations.[4] The Papal decision of December 1980 was privately conveyed to the parties. It yielded all three islands again to Chile but limited potential Chilean claims to sovereignty in the Atlantic. There was an Argentine request for more clarification and after three more years both countries signed a friendship agreement at the Vatican January 23, 1984 which led to a statement of final resolution.

The Argentine Position

Argentina claims the Beagle Channel on the basis of principles of international law which supported its interpretation of the treaties entered into during the dispute. Title to the Channel derives according to Argentina from treaties made with Chile in 1826 and 1855, detailed in 1881, and further elaborated in 1893. The significant principle used by Argentina in interpreting these documents is the uti possidetis rule, recognized early in the 19th century by both countries. This led to in this case to the recognition of the "Oceanic Principle." While each country claimed exclusive right to its oceanic littoral, Argentina reasons that references in the treaties to the distribution of the islands should be made in accordance with this agreed and overriding principle.

Argentina sees the wording in the 1881 treaty as a reference

73

to the Oceanic Principle; Chile received the whole of the straits of Magellan in return for recognizing Argentine sovereignty over the Atlantic coast. Chile renounced its claims to the Patagonian coast east of the Andes and south of the Rio Negro, except for the specifications made in Article III of the Treaty. The Arbitral Court of 1977 saw the Patagonian-Magellan compromise as the salient feature here, but Argentina stresses the Magellan-Atlantic side of the compromise.[5] The phrase of Article III is viewed by Argentina in light of the Oceanic idea, reading "...to Chile shall belong all the islands to the south of Beagle Channel up to Cape Horn..." as a declaration of Cape Horn as the Oceanic divide between the Atlantic and the Pacific. The area to the north of Beagle Channel and "other small islands there may be on the Atlantic," therefore, is properly Argentine territory.[6] By this reasoning, since the Channel Islands are essentially in the Channel or east of it, most of them would be Argentine.

The 1893 Protocol further strengthened Argentine faith in the Oceanic principle as the guide for interpreting the previous treaties. While reaffirming the absolute sovereignty of the two countries over respective littorals, it does recognize that geography may lead to difficulties in implementation and provides for a survey and an amicably determined line.[7]

Argentina claims it maintains faith in the April 1902 General Treaty on the Judicial Settlement of Disputes, but denies the validity of the 1971 Arbitration effort because the court's judgment departs from proper international law. Specifically, it claims that the Court (1) misrepresented the Argentine contention that the eastern mouth of the Channel lies south of Picton Island, (2) overreached its competence in giving its opinion on disputed questions beyond the distinct region of arbitration noted in the compromis, (3) contradicts itself in its reasoning by using without justification two different judicial regimes for allocating islands in the Channel, and (4) failed to be guided by rules of international law on "recourse to context and useful effect," instead interpreting the treaty in a manner that contradicted its letter and spirit.[8]

The main line of Argentinian reasoning uses interpretations that take a more restrictive view of the Oceanic principle. Because the net result of the arbitration contravenes the Atlantic sovereignty of Argentina, that country sees numerous errors and inaccuracies in the implementation of international law. Historical evidence is utilized towards this end; the evidence of Captain Fitzroy's discovery of the Channel indicates that the southern arms were historically referred to as "the Channel." The Court's liberal interpretation of its role and neglect of the important contextual factor of the oceanic divide prompts Argentina to question the court's judgement.

74

The Chilean Position

Chile finds the 1977 Arbitral Award far less objectionable than Argentina. The Award satisfies Chile because it legitimates its claim to the three islands and the Archipelago up to Cape Horn and supports the principles upon which that claim was based.

First, the Court rightfully discarded, in the Chilean view, the Oceanic Principle as it related to the littoral sovereignty. If the principle had been workable, the 1881 Treaty would not have needed arbitration. The impossibility of implementing it forced the Court to look at the Treaty's other statements for guidance.[9] No vertical boundary at a meridian was ever specified since 1810 which would have made the east-west principle workable.

Second, Chile claims that it has exercised effective sovereignty over the islands for years, perfecting a claim to their possession by customary principles of international law. The Court acknowledged the peaceful, uninterrupted and undisputed possession of the islands by Chile as a relevant consideration which corroborates the Court's decision.[10]

Third, the Chilean position appears to rely on estoppel to limit Argentina's interpretation of the 1881 Treaty. A study of maps done by the Court -- after discarding the early explorers' maps as inconclusive -- noted that on a map given to the British diplomatic representative in Buenos Aires in December 1881, the Cape Horn Archipelago was attributed to Chile. Minister Yrigoyen, the negotiator for Argentina who gave the map to the British diplomat, presumably would not have conveyed such a map if it were inaccurate. An official Argentine map of 1882 also notes the area as Chilean. The Court noted that the position taken by the Argentine government presently does not agree with the interpretation Argentina maintained when the 1881 Treaty was drawn up.[11] The acceptance by Argentina of maps recognizing Chilean claims estops Argentina from claiming errors in that interpretation of sovereignty in the region. The case of the temple of Preah Vihear,[12] in which maps of official notification were not objected to and were later considered binding when objections were voiced decades after their acceptance, illustrates the principle operating here.

Analysis

The arguments on both sides rely on legal principles. Argentina's position is guided by the principles of uti possidetis embodied in the "Oceanic Principle" and by strict adherence to the limitations of the arbitration compromis, including its right to void arbitral awards trespassing those limits. All of these are accepted and established in international law. The Chilean beliefs in the principles of the supersession of treaties, in the practice of effective sovereignty and in the binding nature of arbitral

75

agreements correctly executed is equally supported by international law. The effort of legal resolution became part of the dispute
itself.

The principle dispute, however, hides several objective realities. First, both countries harbor fears of being cut off from
use of the Channel and thereby having their access to the other
ocean limited. Some have claimed that Argentina hopes by becoming
a two-ocean power to dominate the Southern Cone. Second, the issue
has bearing also on the unsettled Antarctic claims of the two
countries. The close proximity of the Cape Horn islands to the
peninsula streching north from Graham Land would strengthen Chilean claims to Antarctic sovereignty over a sector which overlaps
much of the Argentine claim. Third, the recently discovered potential for oil in the Channel has heightened both countries' interests in what was formerly a dispute over principles and navigation
rights. This encourages both sides to undertake more aggressive
action and raises the conflict potential of the dispute.

Much of this explains why the mediation effort of the Holy
See was successful in moving the dispute towards resolution. While
the principles may allow for a legalistic determination of proper
jurisdiction, such a settlement is less likely to satisfy both
sides when an economic interest has become a latent but motivating
force in the conflict. Principles will not allow for easy compromise unless they are specifically surpassed with agreement for an
ex aequo et bono judicial decision; negotiations where state economic and political interests are recognized and expressly dealt
with may hold greater potential for conflict resolution than legal
approaches. The necessity of removing the Beagle Channel dispute
from purely legal arguments about territorial claims in order to
allow for considerations of the problems of Antarctic and economic
resources is significant. The mediation of a good faith intermedi-
ary, the Papacy in this case, was facilitated when it was no longer based on strict adherence to legal principles only. Changing
the third party's basis of judgement may be an important aspect of
conflict mediation.

NOTES

1   Article III, Boundary Treaty of 1881, Chilean and Argentine
     translations of the Treaty vary slightly, but not in sub-
     stance. The Chilean translation is used here.
2   Negotiations in 1904-5, 1906-7, 1915, 1938, 1955, and 1967
     have been noted. F.A. Vallet, "The Beagle Channel Affair,"
     American Journal of International Law, vol. 71 (1977),

pp. 733-740, at p. 734.

3   Agreement for Arbitration, 22 July 1971 (London).

4   Letter of 9 January 1979 from Argentina transmitting Agreement (Annex I) and Undertaking (Annex II) signed by Argentina and Chile on 8 January 1979, to Secretary-General of the UN, S/13016.

5   Antecedentes del Diferendo de Limites (Argentina: Ministerio de Relaciones Exteriores y Culto, 1979), pp. 14-15.

6   Declaration of Nullity, Section D, Paragraphs 7, 8; Section E, Paragraph 7. Issued by Argentina, 25 January 1978; reprinted in Relaciones Chileno-Argentinas: La Controversia del Canal Beagle (Chile: 1978), pp. 133-141, at pp. 138-139.

7   Protocol of 1893, Art. II; reprinted in Relaciones Chileno-Argentinas: La Controversia del Canal Beagle, ibid., pp. 7-9, at p. 7.

8   Declaration of Nullity, op. cit., Sections A, B, C, and D, pp. 133-141.

9   El Mercurio (Santiago: 14 August 1977). Reprinted as "The Award of the Beagle Channel Controversy," in Relaciones Chileno-Argentinas: La Controversia del Canal Beagle, op. cit., pp. 117-125, at p. 120.

10 Ibid., Section B, Paragraph 13, p. 125.

11 Ibid., Section B, Paragraph 12, pp. 123-124.

12 Case of the Temple of Preah Vihear, 1962 ICJ, passim.

Case Study 5

US vs. CANADA: THE GULF OF MAINE

The United States presently has four territorial sea/continental shelf disputes with Canada. The most important of these disputes concerns the Gulf of Maine that includes the Georges Bank fishing ground and may also be the location of valuable offshore petroleum deposits.

In 1977 both countries claimed extension of their fishing zones to 200 miles in accordance with rules contained in the informal negotiating texts for the 1984 Law of the Sea Treaty. These claims immediately created a resource division problem over the fisheries and a boundary delimitation problem. Prime Minister Trudeau and President Carter agreed to a special negotiation to resolve these and any other problems the countries wished to include. The negotiations attempted to resolve the dispute about fishing and hydrocarbon resources so that the boundary issue would be less contentious. The long tradition of claiming resources on the basis of territorial sovereign possession kept interfering with this approach: each side feared possible prejudice to its boundary claim through concessions in the resource area. Domestic economic and political interests were ranged on both sides. The internal conflicts led to the collapse of the 1978 Interim Agreement on fishing and fishermen from both countries were reciprocally barred from entry into the other's fishing area.

On March 29, 1979 agreements were signed in Washington regarding the Gulf of Maine. The settlement included reciprocal access in perpetuity to all stocks on both sides regardless of where the Gulf maritime boundary might be drawn in the future. Management of fish stocks was addressed in a separate agreement and the boundary question itself was committed to third party adjudication.

Canadians claim that until 1969 the equidistance principle by which the Gulf was de facto divided had been tacitly accepted by the United States: it did not challenge oil and gas exploration permits when Canada issued them up to the equidistance line. In 1969 the US publicly reserved its right to the area covered by Canadian permits, and in 1976 it noted a precise geographic line delimiting the US claim (see Map 5).[1] In its view, the Gulf of Maine was itself considered anomalous to the "macro-geographic" direction of the eastern seaboard. The US and Canada were essentially adjacent states and a proper maritime boundary should be

MAP 5

THE GULF OF MAINE

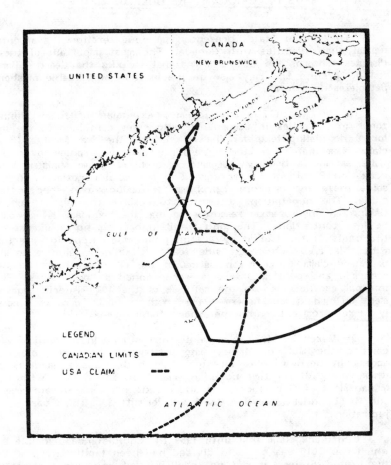

Source: Eric B. Wang, Canada-United States Fisheries and Maritime Boundary Negotiations: Diplomacy in Deep Water (Toronto: CIIA, 1981); reprinted with permission of Canadian Institute of International Affairs.

80

perpendicular to the general coastline. [2]

The American Perspective

While the questions of maritime boundaries in the Strait of Juan de Fuca leading to Puget Sound, the Dixon Entrance below the Alaskan panhandle, and the Beaufort Sea could be settled by the principle of equidistance, the US believed the Gulf of Maine situation should be governed by the rule of "special circumstances." The geography, density of resources, and proximity to major population centers, the Americans claimed, made it exceptional.

Geographically, an equidistance line would divide the Bank and deprive US fishermen of areas they had historically worked. Further, such a line would cover the Eastern seacoast almost to the latitude of New York and the most populous coast of the US would face not the high sea but Canadian waters. The Gulf area is geologically divided by a trough, the northeast Channel, which morphologically separates the 200 meter shelf of Massachusetts and Maine from the shelf of Nova Scotia. Relying on other efforts to use such geomorphology to justify delimitation between opposite and adjacent coasts, [3] the US favors consideration of the trough to decide the boundary. It also urges that the principle of "frontal projection from the coastlines," which would give the larger coastline state more territory, should be a guiding principle in these special circumstances.

Regarding the use of the Gulf's resources themselves, the US believes that fishing on the Bank by US fishermen far antecedes that by Canadian fishermen and that such an historic claim to interest should give the US a right to jurisdiction since it believes these claims are legitimized by provisions in the Law of the Sea regarding economic zones.

The US takes comfort in the judgement of the ICJ that the principle of equidistance is <u>not</u> a rule of customary international law. [4] A state claiming special circumstances shall not have to prove that the equidistance principle is <u>not</u> justified: equidistance and special circumstances are considered to be one rule, with circumstances always important. [5] Article 6 of the Geneva Convention seems to presuppose that special circumstances will normally exist: "...the Continental Shelf shall be determined by agreement between (the two parties). In the <u>absence</u> of agreement ...the boundary shall be determined by application of the principle of equidistance...."

The Canadian Perspective

Canada considers the equidistance principle to be applicable to all situations where no treaty is in effect. Only the Dixon Entrance and Beaufort Sea disputes had such treaties; the Gulf remained, in Canadian eyes, amenable to division on the basis of equidistance. [6]

Canadian legal views changed slightly after the Anglo-French continental shelf case in 1977. This case dealt with the Channel Islands of the United Kingdom lying off the French coast. It prompted Canada to recognize Cape Cod, Nantucket and Martha's Vineyard as legal instances of "special circumstances" and to redraw its equidistance line. This slight revision, 14 miles further southwest, resulted in a 2,740 square mile addition to the Canadian claim. Further, Canada urged that resources -- both fisheries and petrochemical -- should be divided as they were currently used, not according to historic use.

On November 29, 1979 the two states signed an agreement to submit the Gulf boundary dispute to a special five-judge panel of the ICJ. New procedural rules of the ICJ, adopted in 1972 and 1978 gave litigating states greater voice in the panel's composition and the two countries adopted this forum. [7] A judgment was rendered on October 12, 1984 after several years of arguments.

Analysis

The panel decided both the maritime boundary dispute and the fisheries dispute. It is binding on both parties. The Court's decision awarded approximately one-third of the Gulf to Canada and two-thirds to the US. The US received about three-quarters of the Georges Bank area proper and Canada received one-quarter. Neither side was satisfied completely. The richest scallop and fishing areas of the Northern Edge went to Canada. Restricted to a smaller area, the Canadian fishing industry fears overfishing will result, while New England fishermen, excluded from the sector they historically fished, see bad years ahead. The Court judged against the American "macro-geographic" principle and against the regional and socio-economic factors that Canada favored and noted that there existed little clear basis on which to divide the area. Ultimately, it used a median (rather than an equidistance) line, adjusted for coastal proportionality. But both sides recognize the need for further bilateral discussions to manage the fisheries -- and placate vocal domestic interests. By mutual agreement, the two states may alter the effect of the Court's action. Each state based its resource division claims on sovereign jurisdiction but now finds that such absolute division of mobile resources in a shared environment serves neither party's interests well.

The frustration with attempts to negotiate a resolution of the conflict based on principles of equity derived from differing standards for judging what is fair. Resort to a binding legal determination of the rules applicable was a means of resolving the differences of the opposed conceptions of substantive equity which both sides favored. The Gulf of Maine dispute therefore presents both a clash and an agreement of principles. Canada urged the principle of equidistance for delimiting the area while the US chose special circumstance. Domestic economic interests made equal division of the resources unacceptable to the US whose greater population and longer history of fishing the area seemed, to the Americans, to justify allocating to it a greater percentage than a midpoint line would have allowed. But such an off-centered "equitable distribution" line threatened to prejudice Canada's boundary delimitation position and ignored significant principles for defining jurisdiction. As to resource sharing in the petrochemical area, both sides granted exploration permits to national oil companies in areas they both claimed. But each state later withdrew or halted these explorations after protest from the other.

Sharing of sovereign rights, such as rights of fishing, would be a desirable result of a settlement if those rights could be detached from old ways of thinking about jurisdiction defined by US boundaries. The petrochemical deposits and fish know no national boundaries and a mutually agreeable set of principles for sharing them is necessary and need not follow the maritime jurisdictional delineation. Resource exploitation and jurisdiction are two different functions and merit separate approaches.

The two states share a broader common view because they agreed to be bound by a juridical decision of experts which would consider the best arguments about jurisdictional principles in this context. They agreed that the case was justiciable and further agreed as to the authority of the forum to resolve the conflict of principles. Principled resolution, however, does not necessarily reflect interests, and subsequent negotiation of the parties may lead to a different outcome than that which the Court concluded from legal principles.

NOTES

1   US State Department, Public Notice 506, "Maritime Boundaries between the US and Canada, 1 November 1976," (Washington, D.C.).

2   Peter Ricketts, "On the Geography of Maritime Boundary Dispute," Operational Geographer, no. 6 (1985), pp.22-26, at p. 23.

3   The Hurd Deep was called as evidence in the Anglo-French Arbitration of 1977 and the Tripolitanian Furrow was claimed by Tunisia as an important feature in the Tunisian-Libya Continental Shelf case. Neither was given effect by the ICJ, Tunisia-Libya Continental Shelf, 1982, Paragraph 66.

4   North Sea Continental Shelf, 1969, as noted in ICJ, Yearbook 1968-1969, pp. 104-106.

5   Anglo-French Continental Shelf (Channel Islands), 1977 ICJ, Paragraph 68.

6   Erik B. Wang, Canada-United States Fisheries and Maritime Boundary Negotiations: Diplomacy in Deep Water, (Toronto: Canadian Institute International Affairs, 1981), vol. 38-39, p. 23 (monograph).

7   The ICJ was acting in this case on the basis of Art. 26(2) of the Statute and the Rules of the Court as amended in 1972. According to these rules the parties to the dispute have a say in determining the composition of the "Chamber" (or panel). The agreement specified a five judge panel, two ad hoc judges to be from neither of the two disputant states. Ultimately, due to an activated contingency clause, one ad hoc judge from each disputant was appointed to serve on the panel.

Case Study 6

THE ECUADOR-PERU BORDER CONFLICT

The history of the border dispute between the Republics of Peru and Ecuador starts with the Spanish conquest of the region. Gonzales Pizarro explored the Amazon region after leaving Guayaquil and Quito, and claimed the lands in the name of Spain. Administratively, the lands were placed under the Spanish Royal Audience of Quito. This legacy of regional jurisdiction was reaffirmed in the Treaty of Guayaquil between Peru and New Granada (comprising present-day Colombia, Venezuela and Ecuador) on September 22, 1829 in which they mutually agreed to respect the 1810 claims based on the rule of uti possidetis of the other: the pre-existing division of the territory and responsibilities of the Spanish Royal Audiences of Quito and Lima would define the jurisdiction of the two new states.[1]

In 1830 Ecuador seceded from New Granada and claimed as its territorial boundaries the natural marker of the Maranon-Amazon river east of the Andes. Peru remained uncertain of the exact border and, by 1851, after Peru and Brazil agreed on their joint boundary north of the Amazon (running due north just east of the 79th Parallel of longitude), Peru clarified its claims which overlapped those of Ecuador. Essentially the discrepancy was over a roughly triangular area, one side of which ran 500 km. along the Andes, another along the Putumayo River in the north (the Colombian border) and a third along the Maranon River in the south. Peruvians called it the Oriente and divided it into four provinces. Both Ecuador and Peru attempted to exercise sovereignty in the area.

In 1890 direct negotiations resulted in the Garcia-Herrera Treaty which gave Ecuador access to the Maranon from the Santiago River to the Pastaza River -- a short segment of the third side of the triangle. When the Peruvian Congress added amendments limiting the access, the treaty became unacceptable to Ecuador. Arbitration by the King of Spain was undertaken in 1909 and he was inclined towards a border very similar to the Garcia-Herrera line. The militarization of the dispute ended the arbitration, however, and only a US-Brazilian-Argentine mediation kept war from errupting. The King declined to make any award fearing it would give grounds for further conflict.

From 1910-1936 little effort was made toward resolution. In 1936, in direct negotiations the two governments agreed to main-

MAP 6

ECUADOR-PERU BORDER CONFLICT

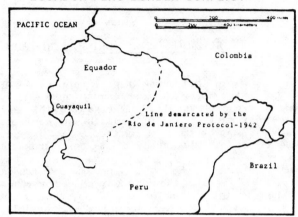

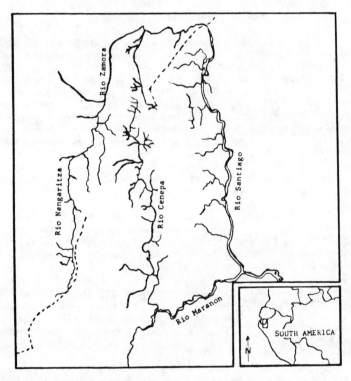

tain the status quo of garrisons in the area. Fighting broke out in July of 1941; Peru was the beneficiary, advancing up to 200 km. beyond the status quo line. Anxious to resolve the matter, both parties signed the Protocol of Rio on January 29, 1942, with Brazil, Argentina, Chile and the US acting as guarantors overseeing its implementation.

As the Treaty was implemented and its provisions for clearly defining and demarcating the boundary put into effect, much of the 1675.4 kilometer boundary was marked by the Joint Commission of the two countries in accordance with Article Nine of the Protocol. One segment, however, to be demarcated did not conform to the geographic delineations made in the Protocol: the Protocol spoke of a watershed dividing the east and west flowing tributaries towards the respective Santiago and Zamora Rivers, but it did not exist. Instead a third river, the Cenepa, was discovered which in turn fed the Maranon, a major tributary of the Amazon River (see Map 6).

Ecuador believed that the treaty had been nullified by the mistake about the watershed, and Ecuador has since treated the Protocol of 1942 as void. Ecuador contends that a new international legal vehicle is needed to resolve the border dispute. The Convention on the Law of Treaties of 1969 appears to substantiate this view (Article 61 regarding nullification of treaties). Peru, on the other hand, believes Ecuador is bound by the Protocol, because the Treaty specifies the border to be demarcated, further notes methods to resolve problems encountered when marking the boundary, and was legally enacted by both parties.

Since 1981, border skirmishes have escalated partly because Ecuador set up three military outposts on the Cenepa valley of the disputed region and Peru sees these Ecuadorean actions as open provocation.

The Ecuadorean Position

One must, in the Ecuadorean view, consider the historic claim of Ecuador to sovereignty over the Zamora-Santiago region. Ecuador argues that Francisco de Orellana (founder of the Ecuadorian port of Guayquil) explored and claimed the land for Spain under Gonzales Pizarro's expedition, and thus has a claim to the region. Orellana discovered the Amazon during the expedition making Ecuador undeniably a riparian state. The new area was settled -- if sparsely -- by Ecuadoreans and became part of the Republic of Ecuador through its inclusion in the Audience of Quito to whose territory the present republic succeeded in 1829.[2] Ecuador's historic right of access to the Maranon River and thus to the Amazon and the Atlantic Ocean is therefore sovereign, direct, and territorial.

Ecuador uses this argument about legal discovery and possession to substantiate its position that the border in the disputed
area should be further to the east at the Cenepa-Santiago divortium aquarum rather than on the Zamora-Cenepa range of the Condor
mountains preferred by Peru. Ecuador additionally claims that the
Protocol of 1942 was signed under duress after a war with Peru in
1941. Peru still held two provinces of Ecuador at the time the
Protocol was negotiated and signed.[3]

There does exist in international law a strong principle regarding treaties signed under duress. (Articles 53 and 54 of the
Convention on the Law of Treaties most definitively state this.)
But duress is a poorly defined word; treaties made under military,
economic or political coercion violate peremptory norms of international law, but the unilateral nullification of a treaty is a
more questionable right.[4] The fact that both states signed and
later ratified the document after all troops had been withdrawn
weakens this effort to invalidate the Protocol. In addition "duress" might not be a voiding condition since such a peremptory
norm might arguably not have existed in 1942.

The stronger argument Ecuador uses to claim the Protocol void
is based on the inexecutability of the document. The divortium
aquarum problem means that a non-existent geographic item cannot
be marked by the Joint Commission. The presence of the Cenepa
River, whose full course had apparently not been known to either
party at the time of the Protocol signing, makes the delineation
of a single East-West watershed impossible. Because of the inaccu-
racy of the Rio Protocol (Art. VIII, Para. 1, clause B), this 78
kilometer segment cannot be demarcated and the treaty as a whole
should be declared void. Also the arrangements in the Protocol for
dealing with adjustments in the demarcation procedure are quite
loose: "the parties may, when proceeding to mark this line on the
land, grant each other the reciprocal concessions considered convenient so as to adjust said line to geographic reality."[5]

Peru claims that the Condor Range constitutes the recognized
boundary and Ecuador acknowledges that 12 border markers were set
into place before the Cenepa river problem was recognized. The
last two landmarks Ecuador has therefore not approved.[6] Ecuador
insists that the 1945 arbitration, which both parties agreed to,
regarding the upper part of the Condor Range does not apply to the
whole range. The Brazilian Dias de Aguiar made a judgement re-
using the Protocol language of water divide, but recognized the
possibility of such a divide diverging from the Condor Range.
Ecuador thus views that award as not defining all future circumstances.

Peru's insistence on implementing the Protocol using the
Aguiar award ignores the following facts: in 1947 the Interameri-
can Geodetic Aerial Survey revealed the full extent of the Cenepa

river. The arbitration of two years before can not be considered competent as a judgement in regard to facts unknown to it.

Ecuador's settlement along the Nangaritza River and its three military outposts in the Cenepa Valley on the eastern slope of the Condors merely represent Ecuador's intent to assert her sovereignty over an area historically Ecuadorean that Peru has in fact acknowledged to be beyond Peruvian influence.[7] Peru nonetheless claims the three outposts are on Peruvian soil. This provoked the 1981 hostilities.

In sum the Ecuadorean position appears to claim rights to the land lost to Peru since 1830, though it attempts to assert this claim only over the Zamora-Santiago region. This Ecuador feels strengthens its claim to a border settlement outside of the stipulated line of the Protocol of 1942, which became inexecutable because it does not conform to the geographical features.

The Peruvian Position

Peru, in brief, believes it has no border problem with Ecuador. Considering the Rio Protocol a binding instrument in force, it believes all disputes have to be resolved within the framework outlined in the agreement. Peru nevertheless contests all Ecuadorean claims outside of and against this treaty point by point.

First, the region in question may have been under the Royal Audience of Quito, but Pizarro left to explore and claim the land from Cuzco in 1542. Guayaquil and Quito were only intermediate stops. The true claim to administrative jurisdiction over the Southeastern part of Ecuador falling to the Maranon and Amazon valley thus belongs to Peru. Further, it may be claimed that Ecuador never had rights to territory on the banks of the Maranon or Amazon because a Spanish decree of 1802 transfers the Amazonian watershed from Quito to the Peruvian Viceroyalty.[8] Therefore at the time of independence and the application of the uti possidetis rule, Ecuador had no "sovereign right" of access to the Maranon or Amazon since it was not a riparian state.[9] Ecuador interprets the 1802 decree as a transfer of military and ecclesiastical jurisdiction, not as transfer or a change of the Quito province limits.

Second, Peru points out that the Rio Protocol[10] was legally entered into and executed and must be carried out. She rejects the Ecuadorean argument about coercion. Article 2 of the Protocol acknowledged the presence of Peruvian troops on Ecuadorean soil by the statement that they will be withdrawn; however ratification of the Protocol was exchanged on March 31, 1943 in Petropolis after Peru withdrew all troops and must be considered binding. The fact that Ecuador adhered to the border described in Article VIII and demarcated as prescribed in Article IX for 1597.4 km. of its 1675 km. length over the three years following the agreement is a tacit consent that reinforces the express ratification.

Third, Peru rejects the argument that the non-existence of a Zamora-Santiago watershed invalidates the Protocol. The divortium aquarum problem was resolved within the measures noted in the Protocol. The appointment of the Brazilian Dias de Aguiar in 1945 to arbitrate the northern sector of the Condor range settles the issue. The four guarantors of the Protocol oversaw this judgment that distinctly refers to the watershed as lying along the Condors; it thus resolves the later problem of the Cenepa River. Ecuador's establishment of its army on the eastern slope of the Condors not only violates OAS rules pledging respect for treaties,[11] but is a provocation. Ecuador's use of the Maranon as guaranteed by Article Six of the Protocol in order to gain access to the Amazon can only be considered expansionist in Peru's perspective.

The Peruvian legal claim is thus based on the principle of the inviolability of treaties. Being legally enacted, the Protocol must be implemented and problems during the process resolved within the framework specified. Additionally, Peru has shown itself ready and capable of defending the region it believes is its own, through attacks on the illegal Ecuadorean military outposts.

Peru's perspective however must be tempered with reality. There is no single divortium aquarum between the two rivers, and the watershed can as truthfully be said to lie on the Cenepa-Santiago ridge as the Cenepa-Zamora Condor range. Nor was the Condor range ever declared the divider; the Aguiar arbitration repeated the Protocol's language and noted it should be followed "without regard to its being or not being in the line of the El Condor mountain range."[12] Furthermore, this arbitration was arranged and agreed upon to settle the border north of the watershed problem still under discussion whose nature was only revealed two years later in 1947 with the survey of the Cenepa River. Peru's own designs on the region have been under reported, some say as a conscious Peruvian policy;[13] neither party is without fault in the failure to settle the issue.

Analysis

On first sight, much of the problem of the Ecuador-Peru dispute appears to be a problem of legal principles. The validity of the Protocol of 1942 is at issue and its loose provisions combined with existing international law on the making of treaties support arguments on both sides. There exists, however, far more agreement than disagreement on paticular principles: both states derive the legitimacy of their claims from the rule of uti possidetis, attempt to demonstrate sovereignty over the area claimed, and agree on the principled process of legal arbitration which they several times tried to implement. Such demonstrations reveal a common base of principles for managing relations.

A closer look reveals that state interests are the true hindrance to resolution by legal principles. For Ecuador, access to the Atlantic through the Maranon and Amazon rivers is a prime motivation; Peru, for its part, prefers to claim all the land and river rights it legally can, particularly with the recent discovery of oil on the eastern slopes of the Andes. The discovery of the two watersheds rather than a single divortium aquarum did not invalidate the Protocol as much as it changed the reality on which both states premised their policies. Reassessment of its interests in light of the new reality led Ecuador to declare the inexecutability of the Protocol when its probable result was judged less desirable than reopening negotiations. Resolution will have to legitimize the part of the border already demarcated while creating a new mechanism -- legal or other -- to deal with the states' interests as they presently stand.

NOTES

1   Bryce Wood, Aggression and History:The Case of Ecuador and Peru (Ann Arbor: Institute of Latin American Studies, Columbia University, 1978), op. cit., pp. 2-3.
2   El Problema Teritorial Ecuatoriano-Peruano (Quito, Ecuador: Ministry of Foreign Relations, 1982), p. 2.
3   Response of A.B. Valverde, Minister of Foreign Affairs of Ecuador at 16th Meeting of OAS Foreign Ministers, in The Truth About the Border Controversy Between Ecuador and Peru (Quito, Ecuador: Ministry of Foreign Affairs, 1981), p. 22.
4   Arie E. David, The Strategy of Treaty Termination (New Haven: Yale University Press, 1975), Appendix A.
5   Article Nine of Protocol is to be practiced as needed in accordance with Article Seven of the Act of Regulations of the Works of the Peruvian-Ecuadorean Border Demarcation Commission.
6   Memorandum, April 1981, p. 5.
7   The Territorial Problem between Ecuador and Peru (Quito, Ecuador: Ministry of Foreign Affairs, 1982), p. 3.
8   Wood, Aggression and History, op. cit., pp. 17-18.
9   Informe Sobre los Limites Territoriales del Peru (Peruvian Ministry of Foreign Relations, 1983) (private communication).
10 Basic Document of the Protocol of Rio de Janeiro, 1942, and Its Execution (Lima: Ministry of Foreign Affairs of Peru, no date), Third Edition.
11 The Territorial Problem Between Ecuador and Peru, op. cit.,

p. 4. (Article 17 of the OAS Charter in particular.)

12   Ibid., p. 4.

13   Wood, <u>Aggression and History</u>, op. cit., pp. 240-247.

Case Study 7

THE AEGEAN SEA DISPUTE: GREECE vs. TURKEY

The dispute over the Aegean Sea has its roots in the distribution of the Greek and Turkish ethnic groups in the Balkans, Anatolia and the Islands between them. The islands are populated by both ethnic groups. The Cycladean and Dodecanese islands are inhabited predominantly by Greeks even though most islands are situated closer to the Turkish coast than to the Greek mainland, and this circumstance is the historic source of strife between the two nations.

The more immediate cause of the present legal dispute is disagreement over the oceanic and sub-oceanic rights that stem from two distinct but interlocking territorial claims by Turkey and Greece. On November 1, 1973 the Turkish government granted to the Turkish State Petroleum Company the rights to explore in areas of the Aegean Sea for oil and mineral resources. These areas were considered by Greece to be part of the Greek continental shelf because they were west of the Greek Islands of Lesbos, Lemnos, Samothrace and Chios (see Map 7). Greece protested, and Turkey proposed in February 1974 to open negotiations on the subject to which Greece agreed on May 25th. On May 29, a Turkish survey ship escorted by 32 Turkish warships entered the disputed area to do studies in preparation for oil drilling. Greece again sent a note of protest, but Turkey rejected it.

The tense situation in the summer of 1974 was further aggravated by a coup in Cyprus, Turkish intervention on that island, and the fall of the military junta in Greece. On January 25, 1975 Greece proposed that the Continental Shelf dispute be submitted to the International Court of Justice. Turkey accepted the proposal on February 6. Turkey's Prime Minister Irmak, however, was replaced by Suleyman Demirel on April 6, and Demirel stated Turkey's preference to establish the continental shelf boundaries through negotiated settlement. Turkey's foreign minister met his Greek counterpart in Rome to discuss the compromis for ICJ submission. Shortly thereafter, the Turkish and Greek heads of government met at a NATO summit meeting in Brussels and issued a communiqué on May 31, 1975 in which they stated that their countries' problems could be peacefully resolved through negotiations and, regarding the continental shelf, through the ICJ.

Due to domestic political pressures, Turkish leaders in September 1975 postponed further meetings of the legal representa-

MAP 7

THE AEGEAN SEA

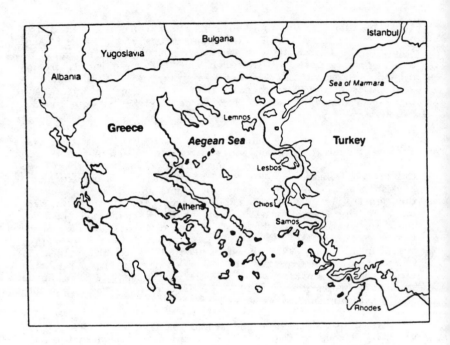

Bold line shows Greek-Turkish border just off Turkey's Coast

tives and explained that Greece wanted immediate ICJ referral while Turkey preferred negotiations. In February 1976 the opposition leader accused Demirel of allowing "the balance of power to change against us."[1] After further oil exploration in the Aegean by a Turkish research ship and with mounting regional tension, Greece asked for a United Nations Security Council meeting on August 10, 1976. Simultaneously it referred the matter to the ICJ.

As a consequence, the Security Council at its August 25, 1976 meeting adopted Resolution 395 which calls for restraint, direct negotiations, and consideration of the ICJ's potential contribution. On September 11, 1976 the two states signed the Bern Agreement, setting up a mixed commission and pledging confidentiality and restraint of action that might aggravate the situation.

Pursuant to the Bern Agreement the ICJ referral by Greece moved forward. Greece appealed for (1) delimitation of the Continental Shelf and the rights to resources and (2) interim measures of protection by the Court so as to halt further infringements by Turkey for research or military purposes in the disputed area. The request for interim protection was denied on grounds of insufficient proof of "irreparable prejudice." The Court found it had no jurisdiction to decide on the issue of delineation. There was no official compromis. Greece had based its claim to ICJ jurisdiction on two grounds: the General Agreement on the Pacific Settlement of Disputes of 1928 and the Brussels Communiqué between the heads of government. The Turkish objection that the General Act's validity had lapsed was disallowed because, in accord with Article 37 of the Court's statute, the International Court of Justice is the successor to the Permanent Court of International Justice. However, the Brussels Communiqué failed to stand as a bona fide referral to the ICJ. The agreement that problems "should be solved peacefully by means of negotiations and as regards the Continental Shelf of the Aegean Sea by the International Court at The Hague," did not constitute a binding referral. Turkey prevailed with the argument that since the two countries had been unable to define the scope of the dispute they wished to be settled, they could not have meant at that time to submit it to the Court. Moreover, neither side ratified the Brussels Agreement as required of a binding international agreement.

The Turkish Perspective

The Turkish government maintains that the islands are not entitled to a Continental Shelf of their own. It portrays the islands as "mere protuberances on the Turkish Continental Shelf (that) have no shelf of their own."[2] According to Turkey, the 1958 Geneva Convention on the Continental Shelf states in Article I that the Shelf is (a) seabed adjacent to coastlines, but outside the territorial sea to two hundred meters or where exploitation is technically feasible and (b) similar submarine areas adjacent to the coasts of islands. While Greece has signed the Geneva Convention, Turkey has not and claims that it is not bound by it. Further, if the 1958 Convention is accepted as evidence of customary international law[3], then the principles governing the shelf of islands, and the principle of a twelve-mile territorial sea of the coastal state conflict. In that case the dispute must be resolved by equitable principles. Even without the twelve-mile limit -- and both Greece and Turkey adhere to a six-mile limit -- the geographic context suggests the likelihood of special circumstances.

Moreover, according to Turkey equitable principles must be considered. The ICJ in the North Sea case held that Article 6 of the Geneva Convention[4] was not customary international law. This article, which suggests the rule of equitable principles as a last resort for resolving disputes about the Continental Shelf, does not bind states such as Turkey nor would equitable principles dictate a settlement based on equal distance. Citing the Tunisian-Libyan Continental Shelf case[5], Turkey notes "the result of the application of equitable principles must be equitable.... The principles are subordinate to the goal." Articles 74 and 83 of the Convention on the Law of the Sea support the Turkish position even though the Convention has not been signed by Turkey; the convention indicates that a delimitation of the continental shelf should be effected by agreement between states with opposite and adjacent coasts in order to achieve an equitable solution. Strict legal principles should not override those ends for the attainment of which negotiations are implied to be preferential.

Turkish authorities also rely heavily on the existence of special circumstances to claim that legal methods of resolution cannot be limited to the statutes and statements even of the Law of the Sea. The Law of the Sea gives islands rights to "the Territorial Sea, the Contiguous Zone, the Exclusive Economic Zone, and the Continental Shelf...determined in accordance with the provisions of the Convention applicable to other land territory."[6] Even with the draft of this Convention in front of it, Turkey notes, the ICJ stated in the Tunisian-Libyan case that it was virtually impossible to achieve an equitable solution on any delimitation without taking into account the particular circumstances.[7]

The special circumstances in this case are that Greece's claim to a six-mile territorial sea would give it 35% of the Aegean to Turkey's 8.8%; if a 12-mile sea were sought on both sides, 64% of the Aegean would be Greek 10% Turkish and only 26% would remain high seas.[8] This would almost completely close off Turkey from the high seas and drastically limit her share of the continental shelf. According to Turkey, the geography of a narrow, enclosed territorial sea in which either state's full exercise of its rights would result in either the enclaving of the islands or the "Hellenization" of the entire Aegean requires a special bilateral accord.

96

Turkey holds that the islands' sovereignty are not at issue nor the right to a 6-mile territorial sea. But the shelf beyond that sea should be Turkish because the islands rest on the Anatolian continental shelf. "Continental Shelf is a legal concept in which 'the principle is applied that the land dominates the sea'"[9] precisely because rights to the sea and shelf emanate from the land. Turkey notes that in the arbitral decision regarding the United Kingdom and France over the Channel Islands, islands were given partial effect for these purposes; in the Persian Gulf, many islands are given no effect at all.[10] The inability to implement the full-fledged regime of islands envisioned by the Law of the Sea without an abuse of right rules out a simple implementation of legal norms and necessitates a delimitation that must be appropriate to the pertinent circumstances and territorial characteristics under principles of equity.[11]

The Greek Perspective

Greece denies that the situation presents special circumstances; rather, equitable principles, in its view, should be the commanding rule of settlement. Full effect for the Dodecanese islands is supported, in the Greek view, by international law and a resolution of the shelf delimitation problem must be made on the basis of applicable legal principles. The ICJ, it notes, mentioned only "islets of rock and minor coastal projections" as special circumstances in the North Sea case (paragraph 57). More recently, the Law of the Sea Treaty recognized the same Territorial Sea, Contiguous Zone, Exclusive Economic Zone and Continental Shelf for islands as pertains to mainland states, with the exception only of "rocks which cannot sustain human habitation of economic life of their own."[12] Because the islands in question constitute a considerable part of total Greek territory and population and boast a vibrant economic life, they hardly merit special circumstances as envisioned in the Law of the Sea Treaty. For the same reasons, they are not comparable to the Anglo-French Channel islands.[13] Greek authorities further point out that Greek sovereignty over the islands is not an issue in the dispute: Italian sovereignty over the Dodecanese was acknowledged by Turkey in agreements with Rome dated January 4 and December 28, 1932, and this title was transferred to Greece in the Peace Treaty with Italy after World War II.[14] Recognition of Greek sovereignty already generally delimits the Greek and Turkish jurisdictions: Greece need only to delimit the area between the islands and the Anatolian coasts.

Greek authorities point out that only "equitable solutions" are mentioned in Articles 74 and 83 of the Law of the Sea, not equitable principles. The distinction between equitable solutions and the principle of equity, between an outcome and a principle is very important for the Greeks. The Law of the Sea refers to Article 38 of the Statute of the ICJ which lists the legal bases on which the court is to render judgement. This is not, the Greeks contend, a license for ex aequo et bono decisions, which can only be granted by mutual agreement of the parties involved. In their view Court judgment on the basis of equitable principles at the expense of the strict rule of law, which would approximate an ex aequo et bono decision is not desirable for the present case in which full legal procedures can be implemented. Moreover, since the Law of the Sea is not yet a binding legal document, any perception that may favor ex aequo et bono solutions in no way inhibits a state's right of pursuing a resolution according to strict legal norms. The Greek position is that the use of legal methods should not be presumed to result in inequitable solutions.

Greece also argues that United Nations Security Council Resolution 395 (1976) calls for the use of international law and the ICJ. Greece continues to assert that the situation requires full legal settlement procedures, although it has been willing to participate in parallel political discussions. Full effect for the islands apparently remains its starting point; it cannot countenance such important and numerous Greek islands lying within a Turkish Exclusive Economic Zone or Continental Shelf. Moreover, the ICJ disavowed the use of the natural prolongation principle as a basis for claiming exclusive shelf jurisdiction in the Tunisia-Libya case of 1982, although one writer who has attempted to detail the conditions under which no or only partial effect might be justified has found that islands in restricted bodies of water such as semi-enclosed seas are not entitled automatically to full effect. [15]

Analysis

We have a clash between Turkish and Greek legal positions which may evidence changes in the norms of proper international behavior regarding oceans; a resolution may either infringe upon Greece's long recognized claim to integrity on the basis of the archipelagic sea principle or press Turkey to accept the outcome desired by Greece because of its recognition of Greek sovereignty and thus the oceanic rights that have come to accompany it.

What are the major differences that account for the dispute between Greece and Turkey? Are they perceiving different realities or taking different approaches to resolving a shared reality? They appear to recognize a common reality: Turkey acknowledges Greek sovereignty, Greece realizes its islands are very close to the Turkish mainland, and the geography and history are a common factual base. They are relatively equal powers; precisely because neither state has dominance as in the Soviet-Japan or US-Canada situation, the likelihood of escalation remains high.

The major divergence in their views lies in the principles they call upon to resolve their conflicting state interests. Greece prefers a legal approach fully implementing the Law of the

Sea provisions and calls upon treaty history to prove full sovereignty and LOS applicability. Turkey finds special circumstances the dominant factor and feels equitable principles should guide the allocation of continental shelf in the semi-enclosed sea. For Greece the ideal boundary performs the functions of binding Greece together, giving its archipelagic geography a political unity. Turkey wants the same boundary to be its interface with the Mediterranean, connecting Istanbul and the Western coast with the world by sea. Refusal of each to recognize the other's boundary needs leads to mutually incompatible proposals: the zero-sum 'Hellenization' of the sea or the enclaving of sovereign territory by Turkey. [The methods used to govern co-operation in other situations of enclaved settlements (e.g., Portugal vs. India, 1960) might be useful in this regard.]

NOTES

1   Andrew Wilson, The Aegean Dispute (London: International Institute of Strategic Studies, 1979), Adelphi Papers, no. 155.
2   Aegean Sea Continental Shelf Case, 1979 ICJ, Report No. 440, p. 83.
3   North Sea Continental Shelf Case, 1969 ICJ, Paragraph 63, p. 3.
4   Stating that the Continental Shelf boundary between opposite and adjacent states should be an equal distant line from the nearest basepoints unless determined by agreement between them.
5   Tunisia-Libyan Arab Jamahiriyah, 1982, cited in A. Cookun Kirca, Ambassador of Turkey to the United Nations, "Statement to the UN Regarding the Law of the Sea Treaty," p. 7 (mimeo).
6   United Nations Law of the Sea Convention (1982), Part VIII, Article 121, Paragraph 2. Greece has signed the Convention and Turkey has not.
7   Cited by Kirca, from Tunisia-Libyan Arab Jamahiriyah, Paragraph 114.
8   Wilson, The Aegean Dispute, op. cit., pp. 36-37.
9   North Sea Continental Shelf, 1969 ICJ, Paragraph 96.
10 See S. Amin, "Law of the Continental Shelf Delimitation: The Gulf Example," Netherlands International Law Review, vol. 27 (1980), pp. 335-346.
11 Husseyn Pazarci, La Délimitation du Plateau Continental et les Iles (Ankara: Publication de la Faculte des Sciences Politiques de l'Universite d'Ankara, 1982), no. 514, p. 321.
12 United Nations Law of the Sea Convention (1982), Part VIII, Article 121, Paragraph 3.

13   See Emmanuel Gounaris, "The Delimitation of the Continental Shelf of Islands: Some Observations," Revue Hellenique de Droit International, vol. 33, for discussion of this comparison, pp. 111-119.

14   Peace Treaty between Greece and Turkey, February 10, 1947, Article 14 (49 UNTS 13).

15   Robert D. Hodgson,"Islands, Normal and Special Circumstances" in J.K. Gamble and C. Pontecorvo, eds., Law of the Sea: The Emerging Regime of the Oceans, (Cambridge, Mass.: Ballinger, 1974), pp. 187-189.

Case Study 8

ARCTIC AND ANTARCTIC

I

The two polar regions have recently become areas of significant disputed sovereignty not only because of their strategic importance but because of the natural resurces they contain. Thus, the demilitarization of Antarctica may be endangered if hydrocarbons and mineral resources in the region prove economically exploitable. Similarly, the delimitation of Canada's maritime boundaries could restrict the navigational freedoms of other powers in the Northwest Passage. There are, of course, significant differences between the Arctic and Antarctic regions that are important for an assessment. The Arctic is largely an ice shelf while Antarctica is an ice-covered land mass. Also, a specific international regime has been in effect for Antarctica since June 23, 1961 while the territorial problems of the Arctic are of a more traditional nature. Both superpowers use the Arctic for maintaining the strategic balance by means of nuclear-armed submarines that traverse the oceans under the ice and missiles that are targeted with flight paths across the polar region. By contrast the Antarctic is a demilitarized zone.[1]

Much of the Soviet submarine fleet stationed in Murmansk depends for its access to the world's oceans on the "GIUK" gap (the triangle between Greenland, Iceland and the UK). Finland's proposal for a nuclear-free Arctic zone therefore was only perfunctorily endorsed by the Soviet leadership. Soviet pronouncements always contained a debilitating exclusionary clause for the Kola Peninsula and the Baltic.[2] The NATO states were also reserved in this respect and Washington, in the words of a member of the National Security Council, was "not amused."[3]

Although at the moment there are no indications that the superpowers disagree on the continuation of Antarctica's demilitarization regime, a variety of factors could fundamentally alter the situation by the end of the treaty regime in 1991. If claimant states feel pressure to resist the attempts of non-members to declare Antarctica a "common heritage of mankind," some may reaffirm their claims of sovereignty over certain sectors. Other factors include the technical and economic feasibility of mining and extracting hydrocarbons on Antarctica or its continental shelf, even if a viable minerals regime cannot be negotiated. In addition, the deteriorating situation in Central America could increase the strategic importance of the Cape Horn route. Not only would a settlement of the Falkland issue then be less likely but also the interest of the Western Powers in a strict demilitarization of the southern continent would be undermined.

Major issues relating to the polar regions are discussed below in terms of resources, legally based claims and policy issues. The next section discusses their potential resources. The problem of territorial titles and the Antarctica treaty regime is taken up in the subsequent sections. Finally, the policy issues of environmental protection, mineral exploitation and rights of access (navigation, scientific research and living resources) are considered with particular attention to the issues of an "internal" and "external accommodation" (i.e. between claimant and non-claimant states on the one hand and between the Antarctic treaty powers and the rest of the world on the other).

Resources

For the purposes of our discussion, the Arctic is the area enclosed by the Arctic Circle, and the Antarctic comprises everything south of the 60° latitude (see Map 8).

For a long time, only living resources (seals, fish, polar bears, whales) were of international interest. Conservation measures concerned the survival of certain species after the overharvesting of fur seals and whales and the endangering of polar bears. Although these regulations were often controversial, they hardly amounted to major policy issues. Matters changed dramatically with the discovery of hydrocarbons in the Arctic. Not only was the oil find at Prudhoe Bay (Alaska) in the 1960s significant in size, but the OPEC oil shock made the exploitation of new resources imperative and, due to the price rise, economically feasible even under much more taxing environmental conditions. The suspicion is widespread that there may be even more dramatic deposits of oil and gas beneath the adjacent waters of the Beaufort Sea, and coal estimates for the Canadian Arctic alone run as high as 130 billion tons.[4]

Similar speculation was fueled when gas was discovered in the Antarctic region. The drilling in the Ross Sea in 1973 by the Glomar Challenger showed ethane and methane traces in the drill core and a similar find occurred at McMurdo Sound in 1975.[5] On the basis of these tests, the US Geological Survey estimated that petroleum resources might amount to 45 billion barrels and natural gas reserves up to 115 trillion cubic feet.[6] Furthermore, the so-called Dufek intrusion (located between 82° 36' south and 52° 36' west) shows geological formations similar to those that usually accompany mineral-rich deposits such as the Bushveldt in South Africa and the Stillwater Reserve in Montana. These findings are still largely speculative and depend upon the appropriateness

MAP 8

TERRITORIAL CLAIMS ON THE ANTARCTIC

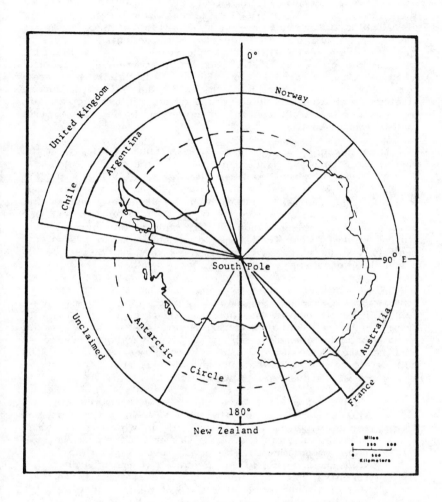

and accuracy of many inferences drawn from Wegener's Continental Drift theory. However, even the most advanced oil drilling technology developed in the Arctic is probably not very useful in Antarctica due to the size of the icebergs that scour the continental shelf, the even more severe climatic conditions and the difficulty of having to drill through moving ice sheets a few thousand meters thick. Unless one accepts large scale environmental disasters as mere negligible externalities, a callousness which, fortunately, none of the interested parties appears to share, it is doubtful whether resources can be recovered from Antarctica in the forseeable future at an economically justifiable scale and price. Such a strategy is all the more likely if the recent discovery of "mineral soups" in the Arctic waters live up to the hopes some experts hold in this respect.

Mineral soups are the rise of polymetallic sulfides from the earth's inner core which are deposited onto the deep sea floor.[7] This phenomenon, which has been observed since 1977 in depths of 10,000 feet (3,000 meters) in the north might provide a more valuable source for mineral resources than the manganese nodules that inspired the protracted negotiations on the Law of the Sea. One advantage of the mineral soups is that they occur within the Exclusive Economic Zone (EEZ) and complications arising out of the need to vest jurisdiction over manganese nodules on the sea-bed in a volatile international organization can be avoided.

While these last considerations deal largely with economic considerations concerning the ease of recovery and the security of sunken investments, the psychological effect of the discovery of resources in the South polar region is undeniable. One is reminded of Joseph de Kerguelen's report of the discovery of a new continent he called South France when a landing party of his expedition had determined in 1772 that its latitude was about the same as that of Paris! In his report, he maintained...

> This land which I have called South France is so situated as to command the route to India, China and the South Seas.... The latitude in which it lies promises all the crops of the Mother Country.... No doubt wood, minerals, diamonds, rubies and precious stones and marble will be found.... If men of a different species are not discovered at least there will be people living in a state of nature, knowing nothing of the artifices of civilized society. In short, South France will furnish marvellous physical and moral spectacles.[8]

The attempts to declare Antarctica a nature park (with a guaranteed freedom for research) were defeated in 1975 by the Antarctic treaty members.[9] The interest of the rest of the world in Antarctic resources did not take long to catch on. During the

United Nations Conference on the Law of the Sea (UNCLOS III) negotiations, Third World nations at their New Delhi meeting (March
1983) proposed a UN regime for Antarctica[10], which in turn
spurred the members of the Consultative Committee established for
the Antarctic Treaty to intensify their negotiations for a minerals regime in order to forestall such attempts at "socialization."

Major Issues: Title to Territory

Traditionally, titles to territory have been based on discovery, effective occupation, cession, prescription and, in the
case of a "hinterland," perhaps also contiguity. Traditionally,
effective occupation and cession have provided the strongest back-
ings for territorial claims. But since the Antarctic is not a
piece of land in the conventional sense and since the Permanent
Court of International Justice in its Greenland decision[11] considerably relaxed the requirements for effective occupation, less
exacting criteria have been advanced to perfect territorial claims
in polar regions. One of the most important devices in this respect is the sectoral principle advanced first by the Canadian
Pascal Poirier in 1907. According to Poirier's proposal, a meridian line was to be drawn from the eastern and western extremities
and prolonged to the pole, demarcating a spheric triangle. While
the countries with the largest arctic coastline, Russia and Canada, embraced this principle, other countries objected and its status in international law is questionable.

Even greater difficulties arise when this principle is applied to Antarctica (as Argentina and Chile have done), since none
of the countries has a significant coastline. South America and
Africa are triangular with their apex toward the pole and large
parts of Antarctica are not opposite any country from which sectoral lines could be drawn. A theory of "projections" as advocated
by Brazil and Peru would lead to further overlapping claims; moreover it is not clear why such projections should stop at the
southern part of the globe since Ghana, Togo and other countries
of the northern hemisphere could project similar sectors. To avoid
this problem, Chile and Argentina propose to augment their sectoral claim with considerations of natural prolongation and contiguity. But the Transarctic Mountains and the Polar Plateau have no
relationship to the Andes even if one accepts the argument for the
Antarctic Peninsula. Irrespective of their largely overlapping
claims, Argentina and Chile have attempted through mutual declara-
tions (March 1941, March 1948 and May 1974) to advance the idea of
an "American" Antarctic in order to combat the British declaration
of territorial sovereignty over part of Antarctica in 1908 and the
delineation of its sector in 1917. They also tried to include the
Falklands and Antarctic in the Rio Treaty in a definition of the
"area defended" in order to apply the principle of collective security of all Latin American states to any British show of force
backing up its territorial claims. Argentina's claims during the

Falkland conflict were, however, not heeded and the US had entered a specific reservation to that effect.

The Antarctic Treaty

In 1959 a special regime for Antarctica was agreed upon and a treaty was signed in Washington. [12] This ended years of haphazard activities that could have been used to perfect inchoate claims of such nations as the US, the USSR, Germany and others, which had either carried out scientific research, once upon a time sighted the main continent (Bellingshausen's expedition for the USSR), overflown the area (US), or shown some administrative activity such as appointing a postmaster for Antarctica and issuing postage stamps. [13] In the aftermath of the International Geophysical Year (1958), which witnessed an increased interest in Antarctic research and in international scientific cooperation, the idea of a trusteeship under UN auspices (floated for some time by the US) was dropped in favor of a regime that built upon the experiences of the Geophysical Year and incorporated the idea of a demilitarized zone (Art. 1) and the idea of the barring of claims that had been proposed before 1958 by the Chilean Escudero. [14]

Furthermore, Article 4.2 provided an ingenious solution to the territorial issue. It stipulates that not only no new claim to territorial sovereignty may be asserted but that any further activity by a state claiming territorial sovereignty antedating the treaty (i.e. before June 23, 1961) could neither strengthen nor defeat such a claim. Thus, seven claimant states (Argentina, Australia, Chile, France, Great Britain, New Zealand, and Norway) are joined by other treaty powers that do not recognize these claims and in turn do not make claims themselves. The treaty in the present form is valid for 30 years; it provides for environmental protection, freedom of research (Art. 2) and free access to data generated by it (Art. 3) and prohibits the utilization of the area for nuclear explosions or for the storage of radioactive materials (Art. 5). It includes a unique inspection system: inspection of any station in Antarctica is free for all other nations carrying out research in the area.

Other Territorial Issues

Several other unresolved issues remain. Questions exist about the status of icebergs and whether they may be appropriated. The Soviets have been using stations on icebergs which have floated in and out of Canadian waters. In Antarctica, the "designated area" (south of 60° south) explicitly extends to the land mass and ice shelfs. Icebergs, however, some of which approximate the size of the State of Delaware, do not fall directly under the treaty's provisions. The delimitation of the continental shelves and the EEZ in the two polar regions is a further problem. It will be dealt with below.

The Functional Dimension: Access and Resource Rights

While issues about territory provide the occasion for the most extensive "bundling" of rights, the competing interests in security, resource management, access (navigational rights), pollution abatement, and freedom of research have all contributed to special arrangements. These new regimes came into existence with national proclamations on the Continental Shelf and the 1958 Law of the Sea Conference and will proliferate after UNCLOS III. Thus, the concepts of the EEZ, of the Continental Shelf, of an International Strait and of Archipelagic Regimes must be considered in this context.

The dispute between the US and Canada and that between the Soviet Union and Canada over the Continental Shelf in the Arctic are the most important ones. Canada argues for the 141st meridian in its dispute with the US in the Beaufort Sea and would thereby extend the boundary established by the Russian-British Alaska treaty of 1825. The US prefers the equidistance principle with regards to "special circumstances." On the other hand, Canada prefers the equidistance principle (rather than the prolongation rule) in its continental shelf dispute with Denmark in regards to Greenland and Ellsmere Island.

Norway and the Soviet Union have been negotiating their continental shelf dispute since 1970. While Norway wants to settle on the basis of the prescribed principles in the Continental Shelf Convention of 1958 to which both states are party, the Soviet Union prefers a sectoral approach based on the "special circumstances" rule embodied in Article 6 of the Convention. The disputed area comprises approximately 155,000 square kilometers![15]

Norway's attempts to create a special fishery protection zone (and perhaps an EEZ) around Spitzbergen (Svaalbard) is also a bone of contention. Several European states have protested or entered reservations because the Spitzbergen Treaty explicitly provides for nondiscriminatory access to resources although transferring "sovereignty" to Norway. The clause guaranteeing nondiscriminatory access in the Spitzbergen treaty (Art. 3) is, according to Norway's interpretation, inapplicable beyond the historical four-mile territorial limits that were in existence at the time the agreement was made. The establishment of exclusive zones in the formerly high sea areas emerged on the other hand from more recent state practice and the UNCLOS III draft treaty. There is an ongoing dispute between the Soviet Union and Norway over the conditions of the coal mining regime. While Norway maintains that nondiscriminatory access to mining, "subject to local laws and conditions," requires compliance with local codes, the Soviet Union (the only treaty member state with an active mining interest) considers itself entitled by the treaty to have a voice in creating the applicable regime.[16]

The possibility of Canada enclosing the entire northern area (including the famous Northwest Passage) on the basis of "historic rights" has important consequences for navigational rights. The potential for conflict became obvious in 1969 when, in response to the use of the Northwest Passage by the US oil tanker Manhattan, Canada asserted broad sovereign rights, in its Arctic Waters Pollution Act over the entire Canadian northern area, as well as a 100-mile special jurisdiction zone to combat (potential) pollution. The subsequent failure to draw an exact base-line, however, left the issues unclarified.[17] Article 234 of the UNCLOS draft treaty, clearly intended for Arctic areas, authorizes the nondiscriminatory enforcement of anti-pollution prescriptions in the case of ice-covered areas. A compromise between broad assertions of sovereignty and navigational rights would be possible, however, if Canada were inclined to apply the Archipelagic Regime to its entire North. It could thereby enclose the area, but would be obligated to set aside a 50-mile international passage which would accommodate navigational interests.

Some resource management disputes concerning the joint management of fish stocks that would require cooperation between the Soviet Union, Iceland, Canada, Norway, and Denmark remain to be settled. The last treaty which dealt successfully with a conservation issue was the Polar Bear Treaty of 1973 which relies, however, solely upon national conservation measures.

Resource management in Antarctica, on the other hand, is largely governed by an international regime and based on three treaties in addition to the basic Antarctica treaty. The most recent and fundamental is the Convention on the Conservation of Antarctic Marine Living Resources (adopted in 1980 and entered into force in 1982); the others are the Convention for the Conservation of Antarctic Seals (1972) and the Agreed Measures for the Protection of Fauna and Flora (1964). There is also a convention still under discussion concerning the exploitation of mineral resources. Thus, through a proliferation of functional regimes, the member states hope to solve the question of resource use without reopening the problematic issues of sovereignty. Nevertheless, substantial problems remain. First, there is the issue of wise resource management because the Marine Living Resource Convention despite its comprehensive aspirations, does not deal with activities such as whaling and sealing whose regulation is important to any reasonable resource management scheme for Antarctica. Furthermore, there is no regime to govern major krill concentrations outside the designated arc and these concentrations are the basis of nutrition for most higher animals in the area.

The second problem, more interesting in the context of its potential for conflicts, concerns the authority of the consultative powers of the Antarctic treaty to approve conservation measures in the Antarctic area. The legal effects of the Antarctic treaty and the obligations it imposes on third parties remains problematic. The consultative powers, secure in their special status, presented the rest of the world with a draft treaty for a living marine resource regime in which very little seemed negotiable for the outsiders, especially since the countries invited to negotiate the living resource regime had indicated their interest in becoming consultative parties. Their consent to the draft therefore, could be interpreted as the required "good behavior." Furthermore, Article 5 of the Living Marine Resource Convention requires "Contracting Parties which are not parties to the Antarctica Treaty" to "acknowledge the special obligations and responsibilities of the Antarctic Treaty Consultative Parties for the Protection and Preservation of the environment of the Antarctica." But the consultative powers invoke as the basis for their rule-making power a treaty which in its relevant provisions specifically relies on the traditional freedom of the high seas within the Antarctic treaty area and which would therefore seem to give all states an equal right to negotiate specific terms.[18]

These difficulties have become even more severe. In the current negotiations concerning a minerals regime there is growing dissatisfaction among Third World nations.[19] In complicated and secret negotiations, the consultative powers have tried to resolve the inherent contradiction between the roles of claimant and non-claimant states on the one hand and treaty members and third parties on the other by an internal and external accommodation respectively. The "Beeby draft," named after a New Zealand diplomat, has served as the basis of negotiations at the consultative member meeting since the Bonn meeting (1983).[20]

External Accomodations

Since Antarctica has a large sector over which no sovereignty has been claimed, resource exploitation up to the shore as well in the deep sea area adjacent to claimant states' EEZ and Continental Shelf would fall within the jurisdiction of the planned International Sea Bed Authority when the UNCLOS III treaty enters into force. The consultative members should have an incentive, therefore, to involve the rest of the international community in a more meaningful fashion. However, the Beeby draft provides for non-members only an observer status. The consultative powers will probably argue that the Antarctic Treaty establishes a sufficient basis for an international "co-administration" to assert joint control over the continental shelves and perhaps the EEZs of the whole continent. The privileged position of the consultative powers is further evident in the draft provisions concerning exploration and mining. Only states that have at least one national mine operating in the Antarctic are entitled to participate in the administration of the minerals regime through membership in the Commission and Advisory Committees.[21]

Internal Accomodations

The "internal accomodation" occurs largely through complicated procedures and institutional mechanisms. There is a Commission, an Advisory Committee, and Regulatory Committees. The Commission is supposed to set rules and procedures for the whole continent, including decisions about the sectors opened up for exploratory and actual mineral mining. The expert advisory committee (called the "Technical Environmental and Scientific Advisory Committee") has no governing power, and only those consultative members and nations that have carried out research relevant to Antarctic mineral resource activities may be represented. Finally, there are the Regulatory Committees charged with actual management tasks and the enforcement of the regime.

The institutional mechanisms are designed to regulate three sets of activities: (1) prospecting (unregulated, but dependent upon general guidelines by the Commission); (2) exploration (subject to the advice provided by the Advisory Committee and management by one of the Regulatory Committees) and finally (3) development (under the supervision of a Regulatory Committee).

The nature of the internal accomodation can be most clearly seen in the makeup of the Regulatory Committees, one of which is created each time the Commission receives an application for prospecting from an operator. A committee of eight is then appointed, divided into two "teams." On one team the sponsoring state is represented plus one of the superpowers (USA, USSR) and one other state chosen by the sponsor. If a superpower is a sponsor, two other states are required. On the other team are the representatives of the three claimant states and up to three others chosen by them. [22] If the proposed exploration or mining concerns areas within overlapping claims (Antarctic peninsula), the claimant parties and two others of their choice make up the other team. It is the task of the Regulatory Committee to decide upon the request and the modalities under which a license is granted. One of its members must draft an explicit management scheme detailing the conditions. Since any decision requires approval by a majority which includes the claimant state, that state has a veto over exploratory as well as mining activities. In addition, the majority must also include the sponsoring state. Thus, the claimant state and the sponsoring state must come to a mutually satisfactory understanding before a management scheme can come into existence.

Although this proposed regime purports to "solve" the sovereignty problem by trading off assertions of sovereign rights against effective veto power, it is questionable whether such a complicated procedure can work. It presupposes the "depolitization" of the issues and the good will of the superpowers as well as the acquiescence of the world community (Third World). We have already noted the pressure of the latter in spurring the consultative mem-

110

bers into negotiating a minerals regime. As of this writing, it also appears that the "club" of consultative members has been able to co-opt in time key outsiders in order to rally support for the maintenance of the present regime. Thus, the admission of Brazil and India to consultative status in 1983 following that of Poland (1977) and West Germany (1981), as well as recognition of China's interest in this respect, may more accurately reflect the sober calculations of the consultative powers about what is likely to succeed and persist than does the official rhetoric in the UN General Assembly. However, the present regime has only muted the interest in sovereign claims; it has not abolished it. There is the further danger that if the regime comes under external pressure, either the Soviet Union or the United States might feel compelled to make claims before the end of the treaty period that would probably make the regime unviable. There has been a significant proliferation of Soviet research stations for no apparent scientific purpose in the unclaimed US and the Australian sectors. An experienced observer of Antarctic affairs has concluded:

> Taken together, it is difficult to regard Leninskaya and Russkaya stations in any other light than as the setting up of political stakes in Antarctica. Druzhnaya has therefore a further significance as the third in a planned chain of Russian bases set up in Antarctic coastal areas to complete the ring of Soviet stations around the continent.

> One may argue that the Antarctic Treaty deprives acts or activities since 1961 of any legal status as a basis for asserting claims. It has previously been pointed out that major activities of the nations which have not formally lodged claims, especially the USA and the Soviet Union, must have some legal effect, despite the Treaty.[23]

Conclusion

We conclude that the Arctic poses a considerable potential for conflict that is connected with the traditional difficulties in continental shelf delimitation, the problems of undemarcated base-lines, the uncertain status of the UNCLOS III draft treaty and the lack of a viable management regime for living resources. Most disputes, however, do not seem either insoluble or in immediate danger of major escalation.

The Antarctic regime has often been celebrated for its innovative solution to otherwise seemingly insoluble problems. Our assessment is more cautious. Success to date (1985) has been largely due to the satisfaction of the superpowers with the treaty, to the marginal importance of the area in terms of their strategic calculations, to an uneasy truce between claimant and nonclaimant states papered over by the ambiguous language of the treaty and, finally to the acquiescence of the rest of the world in the privileged status of the consultative members. All this could change relatively quickly. In a searching article Evan Luard has pointed to various indicators of a hardening of positions among claimant states. [24] Challenges from the Third World are particularly important in this respect and could lead the superpowers to reassess their positions. Even if we assume that their strategic consensus persists -- and the demilitarization of Antarctica is one of the greatest achievements that neither power probably wants to challenge -- the ability to continue in the same way may depend critically upon the superpowers' ability to exclude others from decision-making. Of course, the superpowers could advance territorial claims and thereby bury the idea of a common heritage once and for all. The placement of new Soviet stations may not be motivated by a dissatisfaction with the present regime or by the Soviet Union's determination to change the status quo. But even if such steps are the result only of a cautious policy of keeping Soviet options open, they may threaten the vitality and survival of the present regime. Success in the negotiations for a mineral regime and its widespread acceptance could provide us with an important indicator of the future viability of the present Antarctic framework, especially since in 1991 revisions of the present treaty are possible. It will also be important to observe how much China (and India) can be co-opted and how effectively some Third World criticisms can be deflected.

In case no satisfactory solution to the co-administration issue can be worked out, the issue of the continental shelf and of the exploitation of the deep sea under ISA authority will lead to new strains which will exacerbate the unresolved issues among the claimant states. Sensitivities in this issue area were clearly demonstrated in the conflict between Argentina and the United Kingdom in February of 1976 when the British research ship Shackleton commenced exploratory investigations on the Continental shelves of the Georgias and was fired upon by the Argentine ship Almirante Storni. [25] This is all the more worrisome since, in spite of the presently satisfactory performance of the regime, the dispute-settling mechanism is very weak and thereby makes the escalation of conflicts correspondingly more possible.

To draw some lessons from these observations is not too difficult, even if somewhat disheartening. Many have advocated functional regimes and the "unbundling" of rights as alternatives to the "all or nothing" concept of national sovereignty. Sometimes such arrangements have considerably contributed to the de-escalation of conflict as we have seen in the Spitzbergen treaty, even if they have not resolved all issues. But as the proliferation of functional regimes in Antarctica shows, such regimes need both continuing cooperation of the parties involved and adequate institutionalization for managing the regime and settling the disputes arising out of it. The advantage of the "all or nothing" view of territorial sovereignty is its simplicity: there is the implicit presumption that as problems arise, the territorial unit (and only the territorial "sovereign") has the right to regulate matters.

On the other hand, if the organization of international life is seen only from the simple perspective of territorial sovereignty, other equally important concerns are neglected: the equitable sharing of resources and of access as well as the problems connected with the "tragedy of the commons" (see e.g. transnational pollution problems). The design and administration of effective regimes that can keep conflicts diffuse and lead towards resolution rather than escalation remains a challenging task which is in constant need of adjustment and improved institutionalization. The various treaties of the Antarctic regime have been steps in this direction. The weakness of the institutional framework, however, and its many unresolved contradictions cast doubt upon the hopes that these attempts will be successful and can serve as a new and imaginative solution to the problem of international life.

NOTES

1   See New York Times, July 24, 1981.
2   Lincoln Bloomfield, "The Arctic: Last Unmanaged Frontier," Foreign Affairs, vol. 60 (Fall 1981), pp. 87-105, at p. 93.
3   The only known violations concerned the installation of a nuclear reactor by the United States for its research station which never functioned satisfactorily and had to be dismantled while some radioactive material had to be shipped back to the US. The other violation concerned the Soviet Union. It failed to publish its results from some test drilling in the Dufek intrusion. For a further discussion see F.M. Auburn, Antarctic Law and Politics (London: C. Hurst and Co., 1982), pp. 138 and 242.
4   Bloomfield, "The Arctic," op. cit., p. 96.
5   Auburn, Antarctic Law and Politics, op. cit., pp. 244ff.
6   F.M. Auburn, "Offshore Oil and Gas in Antarctic," German Yearbook of International Law, vol. 20 (1973), pp. 139-173, at p. 143. For a further discussion of Antarctic resources see, Philip Quigg, A Pole Apart (New York: McGraw Hill, 1983), Chs. 3, 7.
7   Bloomfield, "The Arctic," op. cit., p. 96.
8   As quoted in Ian Cameron, Antarctica: The Last Continent (Boston: Little Brown, 1974), p. 33.
9   Auburn, Antarctic Law and Politics, op. cit., p. 259.
10   See the references in transcript of the 46th Session of the

First Committee (30 November 1983), UN December 83-63236.
11   Legal Status of Eastern Greenland Case, 1933 Permanent Court of International Justice, Ser. A/B, No. 53.
12   For an extensive discussion of the various plans and negotiations antedating the treaty see Auburn, Antarctic Law and Politics, op. cit., Ch. 4.
13   Auburn, Antarctic Law and Politics, op. cit., Ch. 2.
14   Ibid., p. 86.
15   Position Paper of the Norwegian Foreign Office sent to the author (mimeo).
16   Ibid.
17   Bloomfield, "The Arctic," op. cit., pp. 97ff.
18   As to the effect of the treaty vis-a-vis third parties, see Auburn, Law and Politics, pp. 115ff; and Auburn, "Offshore Oil and Gas in Antarctic," op. cit.
19   For a discussion of various proposals for a wider participation in Antarctic affairs see, Quigg, A Pole Apart, op. cit., Ch. 8.
20   The Beeby draft (mimeo) confidential negotiating draft proposal at the Bonn meeting of the Consultative Parties, 1983.
21   Ibid.
22   Ibid.
23   Auburn, "Offshore Oil and Gas in Antarctic," op. cit., pp. 148ff.
24   Evan Luard, "Who Owns the Antarctic?", Foreign Affairs, vol. 62 (Summer 1984), pp. 1175-93, at p. 1192.
25   Auburn, Antarctic Law and Politics, op. cit., pp. 54-55.

PART III

CONCLUSION:

PRACTICAL IMPLICATIONS

I

We have noted that boundaries between states are among other things psychological phenomena, lines to which people attribute importance for cultural, historical, and political reasons. The social functions of boundaries are numerous, among them being the division of integral economic units, the organization of political communities, the delimitation of jurisdictional authority, and the facilitation of communication among states. For analytical purposes we distinguished among three different types of relations mediated by boundaries: unit-environment, inter-unit, and center-periphery relations. If we wish to resolve border and territorial disputes, all three aspects must be considered. What are some of the practical implications for the settlement of border and boundary disputes which follow from this study's theoretical considerations? This chapter will allude to history, events, and "lessons" learned from particular case studies.

Because borders and overlapping claims in border areas and wherever sovereignty is disputed are related to perceptions, a change in a boundary necessitates a change in the perceived social utility of the boundary. Warfare certainly changes boundaries, but war is only one means of altering the society's utility in maintaining a claim to the land circumscribed by the boundary. Perceptions are complex, best defined as the culturally and socially formed information and judgment base against which reality is tested.[1] Perceptions are observations of the world that depend in part on the observer.[2] Because observations are comprised of both reality and judgment, they are susceptible to change from both objective sources (e.g., acknowledged facts such as decisive war outcomes) and subjective sources (e.g., values and normative bases). Border disputes indicate a difference of perceptions concerning the exercise of territorial sovereignty by two groups of people representing their respective states. Their perceptions differ regarding the objective and/or subjective propriety of the boundary as it exists, i.e., the demarcation or delineation of it and/or the relationships thus inhibited. Restoration of congruence between their perceptions indicates resolution of the potential conflict situation.

Here, our earlier remarks concerning the role of principles and interests in escalating violent conflict are particularly im-

117

portant. These two facets of border disputes, the perceptions of the parties and the legal and process principles the parties believe applicable combine in differing degrees and allow us to assess the role of third parties in conflict resolution most amenable to a particular conflict situation (as presented in Table VI). It is important to note that these two factors, perceptions and principles, are not mutually exclusive: the applicable principles are derived from perceptions of the situation and perceptions are structured in part by socially and culturally accepted principles. The distinctions made here are for theoretical clarity and prepare the ground for some practical suggestions below.

To start with Box I in Table VI, the congruent-congruent situation implies that both states have relatively similar perceptions of the situational "reality," recognize each others' interests and recognize the same legal principles and procedures as appropriate for resolution of the problem. This situation should yield peace or the use of tightly structured international legal mechanisms to resolve such disputes as exist. An example of this situation might be the North Sea Continental Shelf case which the ICJ decided in 1969.[3] The Netherlands, Germany, and Denmark subscribed to the same mode of continental shelf demarcation -- equidistance lines drawn from the shore -- but this clearly yielded an inequitable result with which Germany was dissatisfied. The appropriate use of the principles concerned all parties and they agreed to refer the case to a traditional ICJ judgment procedure. Such cases, of course, have the least degree of armed conflict potential. Accordingly, none of the case studies fit this category.

Table VI

| | PRINCIPLES | |
	Congruent	Incongruent
Congruent PERCEPTION	Peace I Tight IL Use (ICJ) North Sea Continental Shelf	Passive Dispute II ex aequo et bono, bilat. negotiations US-Can., Greece-Turkey, Japan-USSR
Incongruent	Passive-Active III Looser IL Use arbitration, adjud. Ecuador-Peru Beagle Channel	Most Active & IV Dangerous Situation Little Third Party action accepted Falklands, Ethiopia-Som.

Box II contains a more conflictual situation: when perceptions of the two parties agree on the facts and context of a problem but disagree as to the reasoning proper to resolve it, they lack the common normative framework needed to guide resolution of an agreed factual situation. Without such agreement on proper principles or methods for use in legal procedures, extra-legal mediation, bilateral negotiation, and resolution according to the interests of the parties (ex aequo et bono) appear to hold more promise for reaching a settlement. Pressing for coordination of principles is a difficult strategy; principles are difficult to compromise because of the the social mores that engender them, the honor tied to upholding them, and the publicity with which they are held. Perceptions change if new facts are (usually forcefully) inserted into the context; principles, being standards for judgment, are less malleable. This "congruent perceptions – incongruent principles" situation may lead to stalemate if the parties are well-matched in military strength or if the "plaintiff" state is considerably weaker than the "defendant" state.

Of the case studies undertaken here, three appeared to fit this category: US vs. Canada, Greece vs. Turkey, and Japan vs. USSR. The geography, history and factual basis for the positions held are shared by the parties.[4] Disagreement focuses on principles according to which the boundary delineation should be made. The preference for equitable principles held by the US, Turkey, and Japan contrasts with the strict legal framework preferred by Canada, Greece, and the Soviet Union.

Box III is somewhat more conflictual; there exists a lack of clear inequality of strength between the parties. Here incongruence of perceptions exists, while disagreement about the facts of the case leads to frustration with peaceful methods of resolution. Even though the principles both parties espouse may be congruent -- in territorial issues taking the form of anti-colonialism, practice of effective administration, and intent to govern; in issues involving the marine littoral, the "Oceanic Principle," uti possidetis, and so forth -- they are unable to implement them. This stems from the differing views about the circumstances of the dispute, be it ethnic distribution, colonial history, or geographic information. Differing bases of knowledge or perceptions of relevance naturally yield different results even when using the same principles. The best resolution mechanisms would be those that reduce the perceptual differences themselves or reduce the importance of the parties' perceptions: adjudication and loose legal mechanisms would be preferable here. Establishing either a common knowledge base or bringing in a third party with its own knowledge base would allow formulation of coherent principles.

The case studies fitting this situation are Ecuador vs. Peru and Argentina vs. Chile (Beagle Channel). Sharing a common descent from Spanish colonization and common principles for allocating land, the looser forms of international legal intercession such as arbitration or adjudication making use of these principles were preferred options. In both cases, however, the state had to see the legal process as according with its interest; otherwise, the agreed process would have produced an unacceptable result. Argen-

119

tina's refusal to accept the Beagle Channel award displays this; the award was effectively accepted once the Papal mediation ensured the underlying interests.

The most conflictual situation is that of Box IV, the category in which neither perceptions of the situation nor principles appropriate for its resolution are held in common. These situations offer the least likelihood of agreed legal intervention because the parties are unlikely to agree on a compromis for submitting the issue to the ICJ or an ad hoc committee, arbiter or tribunal. The differing principles probably stem partly from incongruent perceptions. These two aspects reinforce the differences between the parties and create a positive feedback loop that presses towards disequilibrium. Because there exists little trust between the parties, there will be little incentive to trust a third party decision that in turn relies upon the opponent's compliance for its implementation. Because negotiating avenues of resolution appear blocked, armed force that creates objective "facts" such as de facto change in control or infringement of territorial sovereignty are more readily tried.

The Falkland Islands and the Ethiopian-Somali conflicts most clearly fit this category. In the first case, stalemate due to strong-weak power interaction led to Argentine frustration and, having neither the same perceptions of factual reality nor common principles for legal resolution, escalation resulted. In the Japan-Soviet and US-Canada cases of strong-weak interactions by contrast there existed a shared perception of credible strength sufficient to avoid the use of armed force. Argentina's doubts that Britain could or would utilize its strength regarding the Falklands allowed the possibility of conflict. The Ogaden situation is similar; neither side perceives an avenue for reaching a settlement without the use of force, while no clear power disparity exists among the contestants.

Table VI incorporates a number of theoretical perspectives while remaining a useful picture of reality. Because perceptions try to capture "reality" -- particularly observable realities, such as relative military strength and vulnerability to coercion -- the diagram incorporates the distribution of power capabilities. This "macro-context" of a border conflict is important, giving the baselines from which states consider their range of possible actions. Realpolitik offers an accurate framework for analysis if the parties have the same understanding of each other's strength, and armed conflict will probably then be avoided. The hypothesis here, as in Blainey's study of war[5], is that states agreeing on their respective power capabilities will avoid the mutual waste of effort and resources in a war. Accurate perception of physical ability -- or vulnerability -- will set limits on action and set the tone of diplomacy; the reality of power differences which both sides recognize keeps the situation from escalating to an armed conflict. Although Japan is dissatisfied with the present situation in which several islands off Hokkaido are held by the USSR, it shares the perception of the Soviet Union that only negotiated efforts can be used to retrieve the territories. Conversely, the lack of clear superiority between Ecuador and Peru or between Ethiopia and Somalia yields a propensity to try armed efforts if peaceful means to resolve the dispute fail.

This brings us to a second theoretical aspect the diagram reveals: the perceptual variable in the situation can be considered simultaneously with power calculations, not as an afterthought. The importance of misperception in international politics has been noted in the irrational consistency, egocentrism, wishful thinking, dissonance-avoidance and other traits apparent in the cognitive processes of national leaders.[6] Conscious inclusion of these variables may yield a more accurate analysis of a conflict situation. For instance, in the Falklands/Malvinas crisis, Alexander Haig remarked on the disbelief he found among Argentina's generals that the UK would really fight for 1800 people in the present era of anti-colonialism.[7] The accuracy of the decision-makers' perceptions can only be measured in regard to their congruence or incongruence with the perceptions actually held by their counterparts. In another example, the Turkish dispatch of an oil exploration ship in 1974 into Aegean waters claimed by Greece was a provocation that could have entailed a risk of war, but Turkish perceptions of Greece's probable reaction to the incident were fairly accurate, the reaction being fairly moderate.

This "micro-context" of the dispute in terms of leadership perceptions at the time extends to domestic political variables. Although the present model does not provide indications of the importance of this level of analysis in a particular case, the existence of such state-level variables can be significant in the formation of foreign policy. In the Falklands/Malvinas example, the domestic political situation of the ruling junta made the Malvinas war a unifying and necessary action if dissent and unrest were to be quelled. In the United States-Canada Gulf of Maine situation, the role of domestic politics and economic interest made dividing the Georges Bank fishing ground a very slow process. The US and Canadian reliance respectively on the principles of special circumstances and historic use versus the equidistance principle probably reflected domestic political interests as much as confidently held beliefs of legality.

The framework offers a third theoretical advantage: it directs the analyst's attention to variables of principle both legal and extralegal. Legally both international and municipal norms are important and their congruence or incongruence among states indicates the scope and role norms can play in diffusing the conflict of interests. Extralegally, cultural and social norms and values should be included as well as social conceptions of the functions of the boundary as noted in the chapter 2. Legal principles differentiate national perspectives, but so do norms and value systems. Somalia may, for instance, like much of the Arab world, view boundaries between fellow Islamic states as mere artificial and transitory markers within the Islamic universe on earth. The border Somalia shares with Ethiopia divides ethnically Somali Islamic peoples. The impermeability of the boundary which Ethiopia attempts to maintain antagonizes Somalia not only because of its historical arbitrariness but also because of its division of Moslems in a way that leaves some under the rule of Coptic Christians. This intensifies the sense of cultural nationalism and the propriety of choosing a boundary that separates Moslems and non-Moslems.

In a similar way, Japan differs from the USSR in its interpretation of the postwar treaties regarding the Kuriles, but of equal importance are the two countries' differing conceptions of a border. A boundary defines not just who has juridiction but who has historic and cultural claims in the territories. To Japan the islands are not just land to be bargained over, they are inherently Japanese in nature: the islands' biological and botanical character is that of Japan, not that of the Arctic as are the rest of the Kuriles. This evidences a deeper conviction that the islands are ancestral property of Japan, inhabited by Japanese peoples since the state's founding by the legendary Emperor Jimmu, descendant of Amaterasu, the sun goddess. The Japanese homeland is a sacred trust and its borders should separate that which is Japanese from that which is not: ancestral heritage cannot be bargained away. Although the Kuriles dispute may have reached an unwinnable stalemate, it is doubtful the Japanese will ever relinquish their claim.

From Table VI and discussion of the dynamics of border conflicts, several generalizations are possible. They help clarify the role of third parties in dispute settlement (and point the way toward enhancing their role and increasing the settlement potential in case of disputed sovereignty).

1) One of the main functions of third-party intervention is to expedite conflict resolution through peaceful means. This may be done through substantive methods, such as fact-finding or judgments or through such procedural methods as good offices and mediation. Third parties might be explicit or implicit, as noted in chapter 2. Resolution efforts may be legally based, as in the case of an agreement to submit all disputes (or just that dispute) to a particular tribunal for judgment or non-legally based as in the case of a resolution by the United Nations or unofficially arranged by third-party mediation. The critical element remains the belief of the two disputants that the third party can help in the achievement of a settlement or resolution and that its role in both substance and procedure should be considered.

2) The ostensible goal of third-party intervention is to achieve an exchange of promises and commitments between the parties, usually in writing, that particular actions will be taken to resolve the source of the dispute.[8] Such agreements, either legally or informally framed, are the goal of conflict mediation. Trust between the two disputants is crucial to the formulation of settlements; without the faith that the promises exchanged will be carried out, a peaceful effort to solve the problem will collapse. The third party, therefore, has an important role in achieving and maintaining a degree of trust between the parties.

3) To achieve trust between the parties and thus an exchange of promises to settle the conflict, the third party must work to reduce the incongruence of perceptions and/or principles. Incompatible perceptions can be resolved more easily if the parties share common principles to guide resolution; a difference in principles can be sidestepped if there exists a single perception of reality in which both parties can work to satisfy their interests. Progress in agreement on either principles or perceptions will make the situation more manageable by expanding the number of processes through which settlement can be pursued. The resolution of incompatible principles is eased if legal processes can be agreed upon. But when principles are so divergent that the process for resolution becomes an issue itself, interest bargaining usually prevails. Interest bargaining is not in itself good or bad, but it can take useful and harmful forms. The recent literature by Fisher and Ury has noted this, distinguishing between position bargaining and interest bargaining.[9]

4) When the parties are locked into distinct and incongruent positions, the rigidity of the stands must be loosened. If incongruence is to be reduced, the third party must enhance the potential for change among the perception and principles of both parties. It can raise doubts about the positions held and objectively question issues, assumptions, and facts of either party.[10] Flexibility can only come from the disputants themselves, but pointing out problems and raising doubts about their respective positions can encourage the parties to question their own perceptions and principles.

II

Conflict Resolution:
The Problem of Incongruent Perceptions and Perceptions

On the basis of our model and theory of disputes and of the third party's role in resolving them peacefully, we offer several specific suggestions for achieving congruence of perceptions and for coping with incongruent principles. We address the side of perceptions first.

123

1) The third party may encourage, organize and participate in information-generating activities.[11] These may include, for example, geodetic surveys, census-taking in disputed areas, factfinding commissions, and historic verifications. By creating a common knowledge base, preferably with the participation of the disputants, perceptions may start to converge. Such surveys can also have the effect of aggravating disputes if they reveal facts that compound existing problems; the Peru-Ecuador border conflict was one case in which new information led to greater conflict. The details of that situation, however, also show that a settlement had been attempted before the geodetic survey was performed. The result was that the facts it established were not easily incorporated into the prearranged settlement: the problem was one of timing and not of the third party's information-producing role. Getting both parties to participate in creating the base of information from which future settlement discussions stem is one important way of promoting a convergence of perceptions.

2) Another way of harmonizing divergent perceptions is to ask both sides to explain fully and document their perceptions and relevant facts of the conflict. Since the task of the diplomat has been described as finding a firm basis for agreement or disagreement, as the case may be, it is also one useful task for a third-party intervention. The creation of a list of mutually accepted facts -- and of disputed data that can be put to objective investigation and resolution -- can be very useful. Complete knowledge of where the two parties agree and disagree is often lacking, even to the parties themselves. To compile a list of agreed facts and relevant considerations can help make each party aware of the opponent's concerns. One scholar of diplomacy has noted the importance of exploring the parties' awareness of their counterpart's perceptions, of determining to what extent they are informed about the opponent's views and how reasonable they find them.[12] Greater awareness may not mean greater acceptance, but without such knowledge misinterpretation of each other's actions is assured.

It should be recalled that differing interests are not necessarily incompatible, as in a zero-sum game. Actions which previously were interpreted as hostile to national interests might be differently viewed with greater knowledge of the counterpart's perceptions. In an environment of heightened awareness more comprehensive and well-grounded bargaining and compromises can occur.

In a second step, establishing priorities among facts and concerns may be advantageous. This will undoubtedly be contentious but may further clarify to all parties the importance of different facets of the issues. After identification, the ordering of the issues can give a third party influence in the mediation. Structuring issues to recast the nature of the disagreements and thus modifying the disputants' perspectives encourages tradeoffs, concessions, and comprehensive perspectives.[13] To draw upon our case studies again, such a complete airing of the concerns of Argentina and Chile in the Beagle Channel dispute might have resulted in a settlement sooner than the lengthy Papal intervention which salvaged some benefit from the disavowed arbitral award of 1977.

Concerns about offshore oil, rights to oceanic sovereignty, and claims to Antarctica through contiguity of the continental shelf might have been better addressed through a negotiation rather than through a legal award based on aggregate notions of sovereignty. Working towards recognition of the counterpart's concerns implies no acceptance of these concerns but is likely to yield more pointed and constructive negotiations.

3) The third party can play an important role in interest negotiations by generating options for the parties to consider. If perceptions of the disputants diverge and interests must be bargained over, the proposal of new options and alternatives may keep the situation from stalemating. One study of Latin American conflicts noted that the frustration engendered by unresolved border problems often leads to armed conflict when all avenues for resolution appear otherwise blocked.[14]

Maintaining a sense of possibility is needed to avoid frustration over the slow pace of talks and here the third party can make a real contribution. Roger Fisher has noted that the single negotiating text or "shuttle-diplomacy" approach is slow and contentious, encourages rigid positions and distrust, and requires standoff, linkage, and face-losing concessions before success.[15] It is more productive, he suggests, to treat the dispute as one problem and, after understanding the desires and constraints of both sides, to draft an agreement tailored to the needs of the parties that, with revisions, is likely to be acceptable to both sides. Such an approach would help coordinate perceptions of the parties through the process it entails and it recommends itself as a vehicle for box III and IV type of situations. For example, were this process to be used in the Somali-Ethiopian context it might reveal to what degree there exist actually compatible ends (Ethiopian security and Somali land use) rather than incompatible means (sole and sovereign possession of the same territory).

4) Because a common understanding of the situation can never be completely achieved, the possibility of partial agreements and interim measures should be encouraged. Due to lack of trust, common perceptions may be achievable only in increments, needing time to solidify into practice. The distinction has been made between conflict resolution and conflict settlement;[16] the first occurs when the basic structure of the situation giving rise to behavior has been reperceived and reevaluated, the second takes place when only the destructive behavior has diminished and hostile attitudes have lessened. It is this latter form of "settlement" that may be

more achievable when a complete change in perception and reevaluation is not possible. Even though the settlement may be only an initial step and of interim duration, it can provide a cooling off period and growth of trust between the parties as well as confidence in the mediator.[17]

A modus vivendi can bring a settlement of immediate tensions and lead to a later resolution of the remaining problems. At times the interim settlement can have remarkable longevity: the Trieste settlement of 1954 was not accepted by Italy as an agreement that extinguished its claims to the territory held by Yugoslavia, but the "Memorandum of Understanding" has settled the issue for 30 years.[18] Without mentioning sovereignty, the dispute was shelved without loss of face to either party: as the American negotiator said in retrospect of the situation, "Nothing is as permanent as the temporary."[19]

5) One means for changing the perceptions of disputants and for reducing the conflict potential is to change the macro-context in which the dispute is seen. Every particular border or territorial dispute is framed in the macro-context of superpower and regional power configurations which form the milieu in which the disputants perceive the situation. Problems of East and West German borders, for example, are inextricably linked to the postwar division of Europe and the variations of US-Soviet relations. Most boundary and territorial disputes are less clearly framed, however, and here the perceptions of the disputants can be shifted to emphasize the relative proximity of interests. Taking the Trieste example again, the Italian-Yugoslav problem was recast into the larger context of the East-West confrontation of the 1950s. Common aims such as freedom of policy-choice and the great potential for cooperation and defense versus the USSR were emphasized.[20] Undoubtedly the Yugoslav break from the Soviet Union in 1948 made the reframing of this border dispute easier, but such circumstantial events form the background of every dispute. They ought to be used to advantage when possible. Along these lines, the Aegean Sea dispute might yield somewhat to an emphasis on the common ties between the two parties (NATO membership, free-market economies, western-oriented trade patterns, potential benefits to both from coordinated control of the Aegean, etc.) and downplay the zero-sum approach to their shared sea resources.

6) The trust of the disputants in the third party may be enhanced, and indirectly their perceptions become more open to revision, if the intervening "third party" is a group of two or more states. In the Trieste dispute, the joint mediation of Britain and the United States was more persuasive to Italy and Yugoslavia than separate action by either mediator. In Latin America multi-state third-party interventions have a long history. They have proposed peace plans and served to guarantee the execution of treaties.[21] In 1953 when Costa Rica was attacked by rebels from Nicaragua, the

OAS appointed an investigating committee which produced recommendations that were implemented with OAS support. In 1969, Nicaragua, Costa Rica and Guatemala mediated a dispute between El Salvador and Honduras. The Contadora group composed of Panama, Mexico, Venzuela and Colombia has persistently attempted to find alternatives to militarization in resolving Central American conflicts. A group of third parties elicits more trust from the disputants than does the "Colossus of the North" acting alone. While a single intervening third party may sometimes hinder efforts at conflict resolution by taking sides and thereby changing the macro-context to a conflictual mode, a third-party group of states may often influence negotiations effectively and with less partisanship. Thus, the Contadora group met with the five Central American governments and convinced them to agree on various perception-broadening measures: creation of mechanisms of dialogue, actions to maintain respect for the other party's point of view and results of elections, respect for human rights, negotiations on future economic interests of mutual concern, and others.[22] Such measures may contribute to the coherence of perceptions, and thus aid the resolution process.

A high-level US official noted that "Contadora is positive because it helps to crystallize people's thinking as to what can be discussed in negotiations. Contadora is usefully setting the agenda for finding the peace in Central America."[23] The role of mediation in defining perceptions of the problems is the key here, clarifying respective views of the issues and pointing out areas where agreement can be broadened. Perceptions were changed by the realization that common principles for settling the issues existed, although confidence among the parties to uphold faithfully the common principles -- free elections, for example -- has since waned in official circles.

Perceptions are difficult to change, but the prestige of the third party and the character of its intervention can critically influence the receptivity of the disputants to the mediation effort. The methods of reducing perceptual incongruence noted here -- information generation, perception sharing, option creation, interim measures, and casting the dispute in a wider context -- all rely on the trustworthiness of the third party. All measures to enhance this trait should be considered. One such measure is to have the mediation by a group of states.

III

Working Toward Harmony of Principles

Perceptions change as new data become accepted as "facts;" they are, however, also based on principles which are normative at their core. We earlier described principles as involving both the legal reasoning by which disputes should be resolved (e.g., belief

127

in the equidistance principle) and the process mechanisms through which such reasoning should be determined (e.g., belief in arbitral settlement). Such principles may be pushed toward congruence through legal and process methods.

1) One method of bringing flexibility into a rigid confrontations of principle is to raise doubts about its application in the given instance. Does the issue, the third party may ask, properly illustrate the principle? Why are alternative principles not appropriate? Are the state's interests best pursued through strict adherence to this principle? How compatible is the principle with competing patterns of reasoning concerning the dispute? A third party, alone with one of the disputants, can raise such questions and arouse doubts about the uniqueness of a given principle's applicability to the case.

Care should be taken by mediators not to question the base values from which adherence to these principles springs. Questioning values such as ethnic or linguistic unity, territorial integrity, or historic entitlement may easily provoke a defensive, closed mentality in the party. As suggested above, questioning the factual bases of perception and the ideological basis of belief should be encouraged, but doubting the values of national identity or ideology is not productive. The efficacy of pursuing these values through any particular principle is what should be questioned.

In the Greek-Turkish dispute over the Aegean, the Greek emphasis on the value of territorial integrity, thus tying the islands to the mainland is put into practice by advocating a territorial sea and continental shelf for them. This blocks off most Turkish access to the Aegean Sea on the Western Anatolian coast and gives very little of the continental shelf to the Turkish mainland. Turkey, on the other hand, holds that "the land dominates the sea," and on that basis declares that they can enjoy all territorial claims because Greek islands are so close to the Turkish mainland. One issue that might be raised is whether, as the Greeks have insisted, the economic and political unity of Greece needs to bar Turkey from their mutual sea basin. If not, is Greek economic and national interest served by Greek intransigence in this matter? Would not Greece profit more from cooperative exploration and reduced defense costs than from a continuing tense situation? Alternatively, how can Turkey claim sovereign access to all the Aegean if it must penetrate the territorial sea of Greece? If it wishes to protect access to Istanbul and the Dardanelles, could that not be achieved through reaffirmation of existing treaties? Would not Turkish gains in seabed resources be offset by the expense of greater military tension? When a conflict of interests exists, interest bargaining may be more productive than principled stalemate; a third party might redirect the efforts of the disputants towards achieving their interests rather than scoring points.

2) Along the lines of mutual interests, rigidity of principles might be eased through agreements on specific problems. When
the disputants agree on micro-principles to solve one problem
within the larger dispute, the agreement should be notarized.
Progress on solving smaller issues one at a time can lead to
larger settlements; disaggregating the problem into smaller, more
definable parts allows for more specific and appropriate use of
principles and eliminates the need to fight for exclusionary adop-
tion of one principle or another. In effect one expands the re-
wards available, makes their division easier. This lends credence
to the process of negotiating, builds trust among the opponents,
and encourages further flexibility. If the entire boundary cannot
be agreed upon, formalize the agreement on the two-thirds already
negotiated and perhaps the final third can be given to the arbitral process long favored by party "B." If the maritime delimitation issue cannot be resolved, work instead for agreement on the
principles for division of the proceeds from joint resource exploitation. If the parties can formulate mutually beneficial principles for new issue areas, the older issues may start to yield to
creeping coordination. This method differs from traditional functionalist approaches in that it is not limited to technical areas.
Instead, it encourages spillover into all issue areas on distinctly political grounds, for the normative base applicable to one issue may be perceived as having wider applicability.[24]

Such agreement on microprinciples was used by Henry Kissinger
in his Middle East diplomacy. It was a success because it worked
towards settlement even though it attempted no final resolution of
the underlying conflict.[25] Although trust was low and there was
very little room for mediation, Kissinger was still able to har-
ness the immediate common interests of the states in gaining a
settlement of the immediate issue of disengagement. While the
views of the two sides as to the ultimate disposition of the Sinai
was viewed with two different sets of principles, agreement on the
more limited principles of exchanging prisoners of war, Geneva
convention rules, and relatively "neat" ceasefire lines allowed
for immediate progress on small-scale matters. An opening for more
fundamental change did ultimately come in 1978, when Sadat's trip
to Jerusalem signified an important shift in attitude.

3) One of the most useful means to gain congruence of principle between disputants is untying the bundle of sovereign rights.
As noted in the theory section of Chapter I, the state system has
developed in ways that have tended to leave all rights bundled together and linked to the concept of sovereignty. Sovereignty has
historically meant not so much autonomy of action as unity of
rights. Although in fact autonomy is never complete even for the
most powerful states, and nations exhibit varying degrees of in-
terdependence, each state's theoretical privilege of enjoying
every conceivable right within its own territory is undisputed.
Inherent in today's state is legitimized control over land, ocean,

resources, and human rights; infringement of any one by another state is proscribed. While this arrangement makes for clear definitions of jurisdictions, nature, as we have noted, imposes no such artificial boundaries, it hinders resolution of interstate problems of a shared environment.

One possible solution is to untie the knots in this indivisible bundle of state rights. These rights were not always so indivisibly bound; theory in international politics has recognized a "heteronomous sovereignty" in Medieval Europe where powers and rights were not superimposed on each other as they presently are but rather were a patchwork of overlapping jurisdictions.[26] Recognition of full jurisdiction over some areas of governance (e.g., social or political affairs) need not conflict with the reality of an indivisible environment and responsibility in the community of nations. Allowing for shared jurisdiction within the same geographic area, for structured rather than absolute access, can lend flexibility to negotiating situations.

By disaggregating sovereign rights the implementation of several principles becomes possible. In domestic common law, for example, rights of full title (fee simple, absolute) are not weakened by rights granted under easements to another party. Internationally, when historic boundaries are inappropriate for reasons of administrative necessity, they should be transcended through arrangements dividing responsibilities among those most appropriate to supervise them. This does not mean denying state rights but rather granting them or sharing them for mutual benefit.

Several examples show that this approach is quite feasible. Allowing the use of shared border resources has long existed in traditional African societies: 'boundaries in depth,' more zonal than linear, have characterized the ethnic borders of that continent. Due to the geometric artificiality of boundaries drawn with little regard for patterns of human migration and necessary ecological and economic cohesiveness, arrangements for permeability of many African borders should be encouraged.

On another continent, the Austrian-Italian agreements regarding the South Tyrol (or Alto Adige) region exemplify what form shared jurisdiction might take. Having lost the German-speaking province to Italy after World War I and having no hope of retrieving the area after World War II, Austria signed an agreement with Italy in September 1946 by which the latter guaranteed the cultural rights of the ethnically Austrian region of Italy and granted it some autonomy. Efforts to implement the terms of the agreement, however, led to continuing controversy, but after investigations by both an Italian and a mixed commission, the 1969 South Tyrol Package was initialed. The Package provided an operational calendar for implementing the earlier promises -- more autonomy for South Tyroleans and effective guarantees of such rights as access to government positions, official use of the German language, availability of schooling in German for children, and German language radio and television rights. What is particularly significant about the Austro-Italian situation is that Italy acknowledged Austria's right to negotiate for a minority group situated in the polity of another state. Through bilateral agreements and multilateral resolutions[27] jurisdictional matters traditionally regarded as under the purview of domestic affairs were recognized as a legitimate international concern.[28]

This method might be useful for several extant border problems. In the Japanese-Soviet dispute, Soviet administration and supervision of the islands' neutrality might be compatible with official Japanese possession of the islands and jurisdiction over their social and cultural life. Access of Japanese to the islands and the fishing grounds off them could be unimpeded, while the Soviet Union could be assured of their demilitarized status through rights of port and other public property inspection. After all, the Soviet Union participates in such an arrangement with Norway in the case of the Spitzbergen treaty regime. As evidenced by the Chinese lease of Hong Kong to the United Kingdom in the heyday of colonialism 100 years ago, a state does not alienate its claim to possession of a territory through granting another state specific rights in the territory for a stated period. The agreement between Britain and China on the future of Hong Kong initialed on September 21, 1984 affirmed this, but at the same time redistributed some of the rights of sovereignty.

In the Falklands/Malvinas dispute, the principles of self-determination and anticolonial territorial integrity may be reconciled through shared jurisdiction. Argentina could officially claim sovereignty to the islands and administer their postal, medical, gas, water and other civic services; at the same time the United Kingdom could retain a legal right to supervise the political and social life of the islands which would remain self-governing as an autonomous province of Argentina. Logic dictates that the Falklands' economic and security needs are most efficiently met by association with the adjacent mainland state; reason indicates that for the association to be peaceful the local jurisdiction of a distinct ethnic group in a localized area with a tradition of self-governance should be recognized to the extent that security considerations permit. Governance need not stem from a unitary and absolute source as long as allocations of responsibility are acknowledged and accepted by all parties and authority to divide the responsibility continues to reside in one party. Thus, a lease for political management might be envisioned, long-term and renewable but under Argentine authority. This method of dividing sovereignty allows a variety of principles of governance to hold within a single geographic area, which is what the historic accidents of colonial borders necessitate for much of the world. Additionally such arrangements would lend flexibility to the political structuring of a world of diverse and shifting ethnic populations.

4) One method of coping with coordinate principles that remain completely incompatible (despite the above efforts) is to incorporate them in the agreement settling the dispute but not adhere to them strictly. Official recognition in a negotiated text of the significance of a principle in a circumstance in which it cannot be fully implemented may help all parties to find adequate satisfaction. Notarizing the validity of the principle can be useful: it might be kept as a consideration framing future negotiations, it can be recalled as the preambular intention of the negotiation when sub-issues arise; it can help accommodate domestic publics dissatisfied with the sum of substantive details.

In the US-Canada Gulf of Maine context, this might be useful in negotiations. The equidistance principle Canada favors as a method for dividing the Gulf and its wealth of fish and oil resources has been used in many circumstances around the world, even if it has been specifically disavowed by the ICJ as customary international law.[29] Because the United States has maintained this principle as the basis for deciding other pending US-Canadian maritime delimitations and because it is the most practical, convenient and certain way of defining the boundary between adjacent and opposite states, the jurisdictions could arguably be divided by this method.[30] However, significant elements in the disputes do not allow this principle to decide all the issues present; the long tradition of US fishing on the Georges Bank, the proportionally far larger US population dependent upon the Gulf for food and livelihood, the larger US coastal exposure, and greater dependence on imported oil argues for an allocation of shelf resources in the US's favor. The strength and widely accepted logic of the equidistance principle must be notarized, but important circumstances prevent its full implementation. The ICJ's decision in many ways reflected these considerations.

5) The final suggestion for dealing with principles for resolving border conflicts is more a caveat than a method. The use of interest bargaining among parties with incongruent principles can be an excellent solution to impasses that prevent resort to rigid legal mechanisms. Such bargaining reflects power considerations as well as national interests. As is often and eloquently noted, borders are barometers of power at a particular time and place.[31] Bargaining always requires a power framework which tells each party the limits to its capability and serves as the score to the music of diplomacy. Negotiation of interests is still power-based, and it may well leave relatively weaker parties' interests unsatisfied, sowing the seeds for future disputes and revanchisme if the power distribution shifts at some later time.

In sum, equity is not necessarily an outcome from the interest bargaining approach of box II; input from legal sources such as equitable principles set forth in judicial judgments help to reinsert equity into the mediation effort. The caveat is that extra-legal negotiation can be a useful solution in stalemate situations; but the farther mediation moves from the reconciliation of contending principles, the nearer it moves to power politics. Therefore, a midpoint on the continuum is probably the best point to aim for when principles conflict. Efforts to coordinate them but not discard them are advisable.

Methods for resolving conflicting principles in boundary and territorial disputes can thus be summarized as:

1) creating doubts in the minds of one or another of the contending parties that a particular principle is the most appropriate for the circumstance;

2) working toward agreement on microprinciples, disaggregating the issues so as to allow different principles to resolve different issues;

3) untying the bundle of sovereign rights inherent in sovereignty, potentially implementing several principles simultaneously and allowing for shared responsibility and multiple national interests;

4) notarizing principles in agreements even when they cannot be immediately and fully implemented.

As with efforts to change perceptions, in some cases none of these methods may work. Altering the perceptions or principles with which a state has composed its foreign policy is difficult and slow, and still other methods than those suggested here will have to be found.

It is apparent from this study that the role of conciliation in international law should be strengthened. In Japanese society, for example, resort to adversarial litigation is infrequent because its abrasive, face-losing character is antithetical to national cultural norms. Accordingly, conciliation is the cornerstone of domestic conflict resolution, with gradations from formal to informal legal mechanisms.[32] Similarly in the international society of states there exists a natural aversion to strict legal methods which by their nature must declare one of the states right and the other wrong, thus necessitating the loss of sovereignty by one party. Sovereignty is the "face" of a state, and legal confrontation puts it at risk in both image and reality. Significantly, "the Japanese regard a contract as a functioning relationship requiring mutual accommodation to future contingencies by the parties rather than a written embodiment of strict rights and duties...."[33] This approach focuses on the ongoing nature of the relationship. There is implicit recognition that the parties must live in the same society during and after any particular dispute and that the relationship of the future is at stake in the present dispute. The parallel in international relations is recognition in that states must co-exist in the same society, particularly if they share a common boundary. We may safely assume that the future holds as much conflict as the past. Two states with shared borders would be wise to concern themselves more with the larger potential gains from a good long-run relationship than with immediate short-run gains achieved at the expense of avoidable future bad relations.

To refocus state efforts on conciliation, to work toward the reconciliation of not wholly compatible principles and to improve prospects for successful settlement of issues of disputed sovereignty of the kinds we have discussed, an ongoing study of methods bringing about perceptual change among disputants is necessary. Such change is essential, both in theory and in fact, if there is to be an end to or even a substantial abatement of Falkland Islands-type disputes, each of which contains within it the seeds of violent conflict.

NOTES

1   "Reality testing" has recently been noted to play an important role in structuring perceptions. See Robert Jervis, "Political Decisionmaking: Recent Contributions," Journal of Political Psychology, vol. 2 (Summer 1980), pp. 86-101.

2   Encyclopedia of Social Sciences, Vol. 11, (1968), p. 527.

3   North Sea Continental Shelf 1969 ICJ, p. 3.

4   The Japanese-Soviet contention over the correct definition of the Kurile Islands is an exception to the this and does involve disputed interpretations of historic events. The history itself, however, is not disputed but only what it signifies.

5   Geoffrey Blainey, The Causes of War (New York: Macmillan, 1973), pp. 245-246.

6   Robert Jervis, Perception and Misperception in International Politics (Princeton, New Jersey: Princeton University Press, 1977).

7   Alexander Haig, Caveat (New York: Macmillan, 1984), p. 280.

8   Thomas R. Colosi, "Negotiation in the Public and Private Sectors," American Behavioral Scientist, vol. 27, (November-

134

December 1983), pp. 229-54, at p. 233. This particular issue of the journal is dedicated to the issue of negotiation and its behavioral perspectives.

9   Roger Fisher and William Ury, International Mediation: A Working Guide (Harvard Negotiation Project, 1978); and R. Fisher and W. Ury, Getting to Yes (Baltimore: Penguin, 1983).

10   Colosi stresses this in "Negotiation in the Public and Private Sectors," op. cit., p. 235.

11   Even comprehensive studies of negotiating have neglected the role of information, e.g., enquiry is the only informational aspect among eight different forms of negotiating in Lall's Modern International Negotiating (New York: Columbia, 1966), pp. 9-20.

12   Glenn Fisher, Intercultural Negotiation (Chicago: Intercultural Press, 1978), p. 24.

13   Jeffrey Z. Rubin, "Introduction" in Rubin, ed., Dynamics of Third Party Intervention: Kissinger in the Middle East (New York: Praeger, 1981), pp. 28-33.

14   Ruben de Hoyos,"Islas Malvinas or Falkland Islands: The Negotiation of a Conflict, 1945-1982," in M.A. Morris and V. Millan, eds., Controlling Latin American Conflicts (Boulder, Colorado: Westview Press, 1983), p. 185.

15   Roger Fisher, "Playing the Wrong Game?" in Jeffrey Z. Rubin, ed., Dynamics of Third Party Intervention: Kissinger in the Middle East (New York: Praeger, 1981), and also in his International Mediation, op.cit.

16   Jacob Bercovitch, Social Conflicts and Third Parties: Strategies of Conflict Resolution (Boulder, Colorado: Westview Press, 1984), p. 11.

17   An interesting study on partial settlement as a technique is Roger Fisher, "Fractionating Conflict" in R. Fisher, ed., International Conflict and Behavioral Science: The Craigville Papers (New York: Basic Books, 1964).

18   John C. Campbell, ed., Successful Negotiations: Trieste 1954 (Princeton: Princeton University Press, 1976).

19   Robert D. Murphy, in J. C. Campbell, ed., Successful Negotiations, op. cit., p. 141.

20   Campbell, Successful Negotiations, op. cit., pp. 14-15.

21   Many multilateral agreements for peaceful settlement procedures have been signed since the Latin nations gained independence in the early 19th century, though few have had lasting effects. See Juan Carlos Puig, "Controlling Latin American Conflicts: Current Juridical Trends and Perspectives of the Future," in Morris and Millan, eds., Controlling Latin American Conflicts, op. cit. The influence of the third party was notably greater in United Nations and other mediation activities when several states constituted the third party. Lall, op. cit., p. 100.

22   "Principles for the Implementation of the Commitments Undertaken in the Document of Objectives," adopted as the final resolution of the meeting of the Central American and Conta-

135

dora Group Foreign Ministers in Panama City, January 8, 1984. Sections 2,3.

23   *Christian Science Monitor*, January 4, 1984. p. 11.

24   In comparison with functionalist theory which endeavored to depoliticize matters of international public policy and spread apolitical cooperation, use of micro-principles could allow functionally specific norms to be implemented where appropriate, and yet facilitate their spread where desirable. Traditional functionalist theory is well discussed by, among others, Paul Taylor and A.J.R. Groom, Functionalism: Theory and Practice in International Relations (New York: Crane, Russak, 1975).

25   One analysis of Kissinger's mediation effort notes this: I. William Zartman, "Explaining Disengagement," in Rubin, Dynamics of Third Party Intervention, op. cit., pp. 148-167.

26   John G. Ruggie, "Continuity and Transformation in the World Polity: Towards a Neorealist Synthesis," World Politics, vol. 35 (January 1983), pp. 261-285, at pp. 274-275.

27   United Nations Resolutions 1497 (XV) 1960; and 1661 (XVI) 1961 most significantly.

28   A more detailed discussion and history of this matter is in H. Siegler, Oesterreich Chronik, 1945-1972, (Vienna: Verlag fuer Zeitarchive, 1973).

29   North Sea Continental Shelf as noted in 1968-1969 ICJ Yearbook, no. 23, pp. 105-106.

30   The US preference for equidistance in the Beaufort Sea, Juan de Fuca Strait and Dixon Entrance (near Alaska) is noted in Wang, "Canada-United States Fisheries and Maritime Boundary Negotiations: Diplomacy in Deep Water," CIIA, Behind the Headlines, vol. 38-39 (1981), pp. 21-3. For a detailed but dated account of US-Canadian arbitral history, see P.E. Corbett, The Settlement of Canadian-American Disputes (New Haven: Yale University Press, 1937).

31   Anthony Allott, "Boundaries and the Law in Africa," in C.G. Widstrand, ed., African Boundary Problems (Uppsala: Institute of African Studies, 1969), p. 12; Isaiah Bowman, "The Strategy of Territorial Decisions," Foreign Affairs, vol. 24, no. 3 (1946), pp. 117-194.

32   Robert J. Smith, Japanese Society: Tradition, Self and Social Order (Cambridge: Cambridge University Press, 1983), pp. 42-43, citing D.F. Henderson, Conciliation and Japanese Law, Vol. I (Seattle: University of Washington Press, 1965), pp. 183-187.

33   Henderson, Conciliation and Japanese Law, Vol. I, pp. 95; Also see, C.M. Kim and C.M. Lawson, "Law of the Subtle Mind: the Traditional Japanese Conception of Law," International and Comparative Law Quarterly, vol. 28 (1979), pp. 491-513.

METHODOLOGICAL NOTE ON APPENDIX I

- Each state's Mission to the United Nations was requested to supply information on currently pending border disputes. All the responses were received between Summer 1983 and Spring 1985. In the APPENDIX I, "None claimed" followed by a list of outstanding disputes indicates discrepant data.

- Notation of [Active] was made if it could be determined that the issue had been a policy consideration over the past three years, all other were noted as [Passive].

  These responses were further verified and updated with the following existing pubic records.

- Alan J. Day, ed., Border & Territorial Disputes (A Keesing's Reference Publication, 1982).

- Deadline Data on World Affairs (1979-1985).

- Keesing's Contemporary Archives (1966-1985).

- George T. Kurian, Encyclopedia of The Third World, Vols. I, II, & III, Revised edition (New York; Facts on File, 1982).

- Facts on File (1980-1985).

- The Middle East and North Africa (1984-85) 31st ed. (London; Europa Publication, 1984).

- The Far East and Australasia (1984-85) 16th ed. (London; Europa Publication, 1984).

- Africa: South of the Sahara (1984-85) 14th ed. (London; Europa Publication, 1984).

- D. W. Bowett, "Contemporary Developments in Legal Techniques in the Settlements of Disputes," 180 Recueil des Cours 1983 (II), pp. 169-235.

APPENDIX I

COUNTRY	DISPUTES
AFGHANISTAN	No response PAKISTAN (Pushtunistan issue) [Passive]
ALBANIA	YUGOSLAVIA (Kosovo) [Active] Not claimed: GREECE [Passive]
ALGERIA	None claimed MOROCCO (border) [Settled in 1972 but reopened in April 1983 -- Active] TUNISIA (Southern part of the border) [Border demarcated in December 1983 -- Settled] NIGER (border) [Settled, January 5, 1983] MALI [1,300 Km. border demarcated in May 1983 -- Settled]
ANGOLA	No response
ANTIGUA & BARBUDA	None claimed
ARGENTINA	CHILE (Beagle Channel) [Settled by arbitration, 1984] UNITED KINGDOM (Falklands/Malvinas) [Active] PARAGUAY (Pilcomayo Water dispute) [Passive] PARAGUAY (Paraná River) [Settled] CHILE (Antarctica) [Passive]
AUSTRALIA	INDONESIA (Continental Shelf, Fisheries) [Active] INDONESIA (Fisheries) [Settled, 1981] PAPUA NEW GUINEA (Torres Strait) [Settled, December 18, 1978 -- unratified as of October 1983] FRANCE (Seabed boundaries, fisheries re. New Caledonia and Kérguelen Is.) [Settled, January 1982; Implemented, January 1983]

COUNTRY	DISPUTES
	SOLOMON Is. (Seabed boundary) [To be settled]
AUSTRIA	None claimed
BAHAMAS	No response UNITED STATES (Contiental Shelf) [Passive]
BAHRAIN	None claimed IRAN (Claims title to the terrritory) [Passive] QATAR (Hawar Is.) [Situation frozen, March 9, 1982 -- Passive]
BANGLADESH	INDIA (Moore Island) [Active] INDIA (Sharing of River Waters) [Joint Rivers Commission set up, 1982] INDIA (Border traffic) [Active]
BARBADOS	No response
BELGIUM	No response
BELIZE	GUATEMALA (Guatemala claims title to the territory) [Active]
BENIN	None claimed NIGERIA [Pact to establish boundary Commission April, 1981]
BHUTAN	None claimed CHINA (Bilateral negotiations on boundary demarcation in 1982-83) [Active]
BOLIVIA	PERU (Demarcation near Heath River) [Passive] BRAZIL (Islands of River Paraguay and River Itenez, Suarez Island in Rio Mamore) [Passive] CHILE-PERU (Historic dispute -- Tacna-Arica) [Passive] CHILE (Lauca River Waters) [Passive]
BOTSWANA	None claimed
BRAZIL	None claimed
BULGARIA	Claims regarding Black Sea Continental

COUNTRY	DISPUTES
	Shelf.
BURMA	None claimed CHINA [Settled, October 13, 1961]
BURUNDI	None claimed TANZANIA [Settled in 1924 in Anglo- Belgian Protocol]
CAMEROON	None claimed NIGERIA [Settled, November 15, 1982]
CANADA	UNITED STATES (Several maritime boundaries: Beaufort Sea, Juan de Fuca Strait, Dixon Entrance) [Active] UNITED STATES (Gulf of Maine) [Decision by ICJ, 1984] FRANCE (Maritime boundary around St. Pierre and Miquelon in the Gulf of St. Lawerence in the Gulf of St. Lawrence) [Active] DENMARK (disagreement over base-lines in Greenland in the Lincoln Sea) [Passive]
CAPE VERDE	None claimed
CENTRAL AFRICAN REPUBLIC	None claimed
CHAD	No response LIBYA (Aozou strip) [Active]
CHILE	ARGENTINA (Beagle Channel) [Settled, Oc- tober 16, 1984; Ratified, March 1985]
CHINA	UNITED KINGDOM (Hongkong) [Settled by Protocol, 1984] INDIA (Northern border) [Active] TAIWAN (Not a boundary dispute) MONGOLIA (Boundary demarcation) [Settled, December 1962] SOVIET UNION (Manchuria, Amur River and Sinkiang) [Active] JAPAN (Senkaku Is.) [Passive] VIET NAM (Common Frontier, Territorial Waters in Gulf of Tonkin, Parcel Is., Spratly Is.) [Active] NEPAL (Border demarcated) [Settled,

141

COUNTRY	DISPUTES
	October 16, 1961] [Has no proper base-lines in South China Sea]
COLOMBIA	No response VENEZUELA (Gulf of Venezuela, Los Monjes Islands) [Passive] VENEZUELA (Boundary demarcation) [Began in 1982] NICARAGUA (Disputes the Quita Sueno Bank, Providencia and San Andrés Archipelago in the Carribbean) [Passive]
CONGO	None claimed but demarcartion needed
COSTA RICA	No response
CUBA	None claimed UNITED STATES (Guantanamo) [Potential]
CYPRUS	None claimed GREECE-TURKEY (Claims to it) [Active]
CZECHOSLOVAKIA	None claimed
DEMOCRATIC KAMPUCHEA	VIET NAM (Presently occupied by Viet Nam forces) [Active]
DEMOCRATIC YEMEN	OMAN (Dhofar region -- Committee set up to discuss border problems, January 1983) [Active] SAUDI ARABIA (Discovery of oil at Yemen border) [Potential] Not claimed: YEMEN REPUBLIC (Efforts to normalize relations in November 1982) [Active]
DENMARK	CANADA (Disagreement over base-lines in Greenland) [Passive] SWEDEN (Continental Shelf, Fishing zones) [Settled, October 29, 1983] POLAND, GDR, NORWAY and ICELAND (Sea boundaries)
DJIBOUTI	No response SOMALIA (Somalia claims title to the territory) [Passive]
DOMINICA	No response

COUNTRY	DISPUTES
DOMINICAN REPUBLIC	BAHAMAS (Fishing zones, Continental Shelf)
ECUADOR	PERU (Border demarcation) [Active]
EGYPT	None claimed ISRAEL (Claim over Taba, 4-acre beach resort on the Gulf of Aqaba, January 1985) [Active]
EL SALVADOR	None claimed HONDURAS (Boundary demarcation) [Treaty under implementation, 1980] GUATEMALA [Treaty 1938]
EQUATORIAL GUINEA	No response
ETHIOPIA	None claimed SOMALIA (Ogaden Region) [Active]
FEDERAL REPUBLIC OF GERMANY	GERMAN DEMOCRATIC REPUBLIC (Unsettled boundaries, but treaties concluded re. status quo, December 21, 1972) [Delimitation in progress on Elbe River, German Bay] POLAND (Unsettled boundaries, but treaties concluded re. status quo, November 20, 1970) SOVIET UNION (Unsettled boundaries, but treaties concluded re. status quo, August 12, 1970)
FIJI	None claimed FRANCE (New Caledonia Islands) [Settled, 1982]
FINLAND	SWEDEN (Aaland Is.) [1947 -- demilitarized the Island which remained Finnish] SOVIET UNION and SWEDEN (Continental Shelf)
FRANCE	MALAGASY (Claims to Europa, Bassas da India, Juan de Nova, and joint claim with Comoros Is. over Glorieuses Is.) [Active] MAURITIUS (Claims to Tromelin Is.)

COUNTRY	DISPUTES
	[Passive] COMOROS Is. (Mayotte) [Passive]
GABON	None claimed EQUATORIAL GUINEA (Boundary demarcation) [Settled, 1974]
GAMBIA	No response
GERMAN DEMO- CRATIC REPUBLIC	FEDERAL REPUBLIC OF GERMANY (unsettled boundaries, but treaties concluded re. status quo, December 21, 1972) [Delimitation in progress on Elbe river, German Bay] POLAND (border) [Settled by Treaty, July 6, 1970]
GHANA	None claimed TOGO (Territorial dispute) [Active]
GREECE	TURKEY (Aegean Sea, Continental Shelf and resources) [Active] CYPRUS-question [Active] (Not claimed)
GRENADA	No response
GUATEMALA	UNITED KINGDOM (re. Belize Independence in 1981) BELIZE (Guatemala refuses to accept its independence) [Active]
GUINEA	No response GUNINEA-BISSAU (Maritime Boundary) [Settled by ICJ, February 1985]
GUINEA-BISSAU	No response GUNINEA (Maritime Boundary) [Settled by ICJ, February 1985]
GUYANA	No response VENEZUELA (Seized and fortified Anakoko Islands, on the Cuyuni River, and claims west of the Essequibo River) [12 year moratorium in 1970; 1982 negotiations on settlement, asked the Secretary-General for mediation -- Active] SURINAME (Territory between Corentyne River and the New River; largely

144

COUNTRY	DISPUTES
	uninhabited area under Guyanese control) [1970 agreement to demilitarize, not implemented yet -- Passive]
HAITI	No response UNITED STATES (Navassa Island) [Reactivated, 1981 -- Passive]
HONDURAS	EL SALVADOR (Boundary demarcation) [Lima peace treaty (1980) under implementation] NICARAGUA (Mosquito Coast) [Decision by ICJ, 1960]
HUNGARY	None claimed
ICELAND	None claimed
INDIA	CHINA (Aksi Chin, NEFA region, Sikkim border) [Active] PAKISTAN (Rann of Kutch) [Settled, 1968] PAKISTAN (Kashmir) [Passive] BANGLADESH (New Moore Is.) [Active] BANGLADESH (Sharing of River Waters) [Joint Rivers Commission set up, 1982]
INDONESIA	None claimed MALAYSIA & THAILAND [Continental Shelf Pact 1979] MALAYSIA (Maritime treaty recognized Jakarta's "archipelagic principle") [Settled, February 25, 1982] THAILAND (Northern part of Straits of Malacca and in the Andaman Sea) [Agreement] PAPUA NEW GUINEA [Agreement] SINGAPORE (Territorial Seas in the Strait of Singapore) [Agreement] AUSTRALIA (on Seabed boundaries in the area of the Timor and Arafura Seas) [Agreement claimed; Australia claims issues under negotiation, only issue of fisheries settled in 1981] Not claimed: EAST TIMOR (Right to Self-determination) [Active]
IRAN	No response IRAQ (Shatt-al-Arab waterways) [Active] UAE (Abu Musa and the Lesser Tunb Is.)

COUNTRY	DISPUTES
	[Iraq has claimed it on behalf of the UAE in the present war in the Gulf -- Active]
	BAHRAIN (Iran claims title to the territory -- Settled in 1970; revived in 1979) [Passive]
IRAQ	No response
	IRAN (Shatt-al-Arab waterways) [Active]
	KUWAIT (Dispute over Warba and Bubiyan Is.) [Passive]
IRELAND	UNITED KINGDOM (Northern Irish issue) [Active]
	UNITED KINGDOM (Continental Shelf)
ISRAEL	Claim disengagement agreements and peace treaty
	SYRIA, JORDAN (Territorial dispute) [Active]
	EGYPT [Treaty on procedures for resolving Boundary questions, April 1982; Dispute over Taba, 4-acre beach resort on the Gulf of Aqaba, controlled by Israel -- Active]
ITALY	YUGOSLAVIA (Trieste) [Settled, 1975 -- Treaty of Osimo]
	GREECE (Continental Shelf) [Settled, May 24, 1977]
	SPAIN (Continental Shelf) [Settled, February 19, 1974]
	TUNISIA (Continental Shelf) [Settled, August 20, 1971]
	YUGOSLAVIA (Continental Shelf) [Settled, January 8, 1968]
	FRANCE, LIBYA, ALGERIA, MALTA and ALBANIA (Maritime boundaries undetermined in the Mediterranean)
IVORY COAST	None claimed
JAMAICA	None claimed
JAPAN	USSR (Northern Territories) [Passive]
	CHINA (Senkaku Islands [Passive]
	UNITED STATES (Okinawa) [Returned -- Settled]

COUNTRY	DISPUTES
JORDAN	ISRAEL (Territorial dispute) [Active]
KENYA	None claimed SUDAN (No dispute claimed but delineation of Sudanese border needed) TANZANIA [Settled, November-December 1983] SOMALIA (Continental Shelf) [Agreement to cooperate, June 1981]
KUWAIT	IRAQ (Bilateral talks on border delineation; claims to Warba and Bubiyan Is.) [Passive] Not claimed: SAUDI ARABIA (Neutral zone) [Agreement on the distribution of oil resources -- Passive]
LAOS	THAILAND (Parts of Laos claimed) [Active] Not claimed: VIET NAM (historical) [Active]
LEBANON	None claimed ISRAEL (Treaty unimplemented) [Active] [Foreign occupation of parts of the country]
LESOTHO	SOUTH AFRICA [Passive]
LIBERIA	None claimed
LIBYA	None claimed CHAD (Aozou Strip) [Active] TUNISIA (Mineral rights in the oil rich Continental Shelf) [Settled by ICJ, February 23, 1982; Re-erupted on February 27, 1982 -- Active] MALTA (Continental Shelf) [Delimited by ICJ, 1985]
LUXEMBOURG	None claimed
MALAGASY (MADAGASCAR)	FRANCE (Dispute over Juan de Nova, Europa, Bassas de India, and the Glorieuses) [Active]
MALAWI	None claimed TANZANIA (Lake Nyasa) [Partial rapproachment since 1972]

COUNTRY	DISPUTES
MALAYSIA	INDONESIA-BORNEO (Maritime treaty) [Settled, 1982]
	PHILIPPINES (Sabah) [Settled, 1977]
	THAILAND (Continental Shelf) [Question of joint exploitation -- Settled in 1979; raised in 1980 as it was not reflected in the Malaysian map]
	SINGAPORE (Water resource use) [Agreement, August 1982]
	Not claimed: SINGAPORE (claims over the Is. of Pulau Batu Putch/Pedra Branca in the Strait of Singapore) [Agreed to negotiate]
	SPRATLY Island of Terumbu Layang (Claimed and occupied in 1983) [Active]
	VIET NAM (claims to Reef of Pulau Kecil Amboyna, north of Sabah -- occupied by Viet Nam troops; claims triangular area off the Kelantan coast which was the subject of MALAYSIA-THAILAND agreement in 1979)
MALDIVES	None claimed
MALI	ALGERIA, UPPER VOLTA, MAURITANIA, and NIGER [New boundary Agreements, 1983]
MALTA	LIBYA (Continental Shelf) [Settled by ICJ, 1985]
MAURITANIA	None claimed
	MOROCCO (Western Sahara issue) [Relinquished claims in 1979]
MAURITIUS	MALAGASY REPUBLIC (Question re. Continental Shelf)
	Not claimed: UNITED KINGDOM (Diego Garcia) [Passive]
	FRANCE (Tromelin Is. -- claimed in 1976) [Passive]
MEXICO	None claimed
MONGOLIA	None claimed
	USSR (Boundary demarcation) [Settled, 1976]
	CHINA [Settled, 1962]
MOROCCO	WESTERN SAHARA question (war with

COUNTRY	DISPUTES
	guerrillas -- now termed as was with Algeria, January 1985) [Active] Not claimed: LIBYA [Accord to establish, in principle, a "union of states" between the two countries, February 1985] SPAIN (Spanish Sahara) [Ceded in 1979] SPAIN (Dispute over Ceuta and Melilla on Morocco's coast, reported in September 1985) [Potential]
MOZAMBIQUE	No response
NEPAL	None Claimed CHINA (Tibet boundary) [Settled, October 16, 1961]
NETHERLANDS	None claimed NETHERLANDS ANTILLES-VENEZUELA (Boundary treaty) [Settled, March 31, 1978]
NEW ZEALAND	UNITED KINGDOM, FRANCE, NORWAY and AUSTRALIA (Antarctic claims)
NICARAGUA	No response COLOMBIA (Disputes the Quita Sueno Bank, Providencia and San Andrés Archipelago in the Carribbean) [Passive]
NIGER	ALGERIA [Demarcation in progress] MALI (Boundary demarcation) [Settled, 1983] UPPER VOLTA [Borders under negotiation]
NIGERIA	CAMEROONS (Continental Shelf) [Being demarcated] BENIN [Pact to establish boundary Commission]
NORTH KOREA	No response SOUTH KOREA (Not a boundary dispute)
NORWAY	SOVIET UNION (Continental Shelf and fisheries of Barents Sea) DENMARK (Jan Mayen) [Settled on the basis of US conciliation, 1981] DENMARK (Greenland Continental shelf and Fisheries) ICELAND (fisheries) [Settled, May 1980]

COUNTRY	DISPUTES
OMAN	UNITED ARAB EMIRATES [Settled, 1981] SOUTH YEMEN (Dhofar region) [Improvement in relations, 1982-83 -- Active]
PAKISTAN	AFGHANISTAN (Duran Line) [Passive] INDIA (Kashmir) [Passive] INDIA (Rann of Kutch) [Settled, 1968] CHINA (Boundary demarcation) [Settled, 1963]
PANAMA	None claimed COLOMBIA (Continental Shelf) [Settled, November 1977] COSTA RICA (Continental Shelf) [Settled, December 1982]
PAPUA NEW GUINEA	None claimed AUSTRALIA (Torres Strait treaty) [Settled, December 1978 -- unratified as of October 1983]
PARAGUAY	None claimed BRAZIL (River resource use, Paraguay river) [Settled] ARGENTINA (River resource use, Paraná river) [Settled] Not claimed: ARGENTINA (Pilcomayo Water dispute) [Passive]
PERU	ECUADOR (Border demarcation) [Active]
PHILIPPINES	No response MALAYSIA (Sabah) [Settled, 1977] SPRATLY Is. [Passive]
POLAND	None claimed FEDERAL REPUBLIC OF GERMANY (Border issues) [Settled by Treaty, November 1970]
PORTUGAL	None claimed
QATAR	No response BAHRAIN (Hawar Is.) [Situation frozen, March 9, 1982 -- Passive]
ROMANIA	None claimed
RWANDA	No response

COUNTRY	DISPUTES
SAINT LUCIA	None claimed
ST. VINCENT & GRENADINES	No response
SAMOA	None claimed
SAO TOME & PRINCIPE	None claimed
SAUDI ARABIA	None claimed SOUTH YEMEN (Discovery of oil field on the North Yemen/Saudi border, 1984) [Potential] IRAQ (Division of the Neutral Zone) [Defined border in 1981] KUWAIT (Neutral zone not demarcated) [Agreement on the distribution of oil resources -- Passive]
SENEGAL	No response
SEYCHELLES	None claimed
SIERRA LEONE	None claimed
SINGAPORE	No response MALAYSIA (Continental Shelf re. Pedra Branca)
SOMALIA	ETHIOPIA (Ogaden Region) [Active] DJIBOUTI (Somalia claims title to the territory) [Passive]
SOUTH AFRICA	LESOTHO [Passive] Not claimed: NAMIBIA (no proper boundary dispute) [Active] SWAZILAND [Talks in process]
SOUTH KOREA	No response NORTH KOREA (Not a boundary diapute)
SOVIET UNION	No response CHINA (Manchuria, Amur river, Sinkiang) [Active] MONGOLIA (Boundary demarcation) [Settled, 1976] JAPAN (Kurile Is.) [Passive]

COUNTRY	DISPUTES
SPAIN	None claimed UNITED KINGDOM (Gibraltar) [Passive]
SRI LANKA	None claimed
SUDAN	None claimed KENYA (delimitation needed although no dispute claimed) [Passive]
SURINAME	GUYANA (Continental Shelf) GUYANA (territory between Corentyne River and New River) [1970 treaty to demilitarize the disputed land, not implemented -- Passive]
SWAZILAND	SOUTH AFRICA [Boundary adjustment talks in process]
SWEDEN	FINLAND (Aaland Is. and Continental Shelf) [Active] SOVIET UNION (Continental Shelf)
SWITZERLAND	No response
SYRIAN ARAB REPUBLIC	No response ISRAEL (Territorial dispute) [Active]
TANZANIA	None claimed MALAWI (Lake Nyassa Border) [Partial rapproachment since 1972] KENYA (Border traffic) [Normalized, November-December 1983]
THAILAND	None claimed CAMBODIA [Settled, 1982] MALAYSIA (Continental Shelf) LAOS (Claims to parts of it) [Active]
TOGO	No response GHANA (Territorial dispute) [Active]
TRINIDAD & TOBAGO	No response
TUNISIA	No response ALGERIA (Border demarcated) [Settled, December 1983]
TURKEY	GREECE (Aegean Sea) [Active]

COUNTRY	DISPUTES
	Not claimed: CYPRUS question [Active]
UGANDA	None claimed

UNITED ARAB EMIRATES	No response
	DUBAI-SHARJAH (Boundary dispute)
	   [Settled, 1980]
	IRAN (Greater and Lesser Tunb Is.)
	   [Passive]

UNITED KINGDOM	ARGENTINA (Falkland) [Active]
	CHINA (Hongkong) [Settled, 1984]
	Not claimed: SPAIN (Gibraltar) [Passive]
	MAURITIUS (Diego Garcia) [Passive]
	IRELAND (Territorial dispute) [Active]
	IRELAND (Continental Shelf) [Pending,
	   compromis for arbitration not yet
	   signed]

UNITED STATES OF AMERICA	CANADA (Beaufort Sea, Dixon Entrance,
	   Juan de Fuca Strait) [Active]
	CANADA (Gulf of Maine) [Decision by ICJ,
	   1984]
	BAHAMAS (Continental Shelf)
	ARCTIC claim
	Not claimed: CUBA (Guantanamo)
	   [Potential]

UPPER VOLTA	MALI (Burkina Faso) [Submitted to ICJ, Active]
URUGUAY	None claimed

VENEZUELA	COLOMBIA (Continental Shelf)
	COLOMBIA (Boundary demarcation) [Began in
	   1982]
	GUYANA (Anakoko Is., claims to west of
	   Essequibo River) [Asked the Secretary-
	   General for mediation -- Active]

VIET NAM	CHINA (Common Frontier, Territorial
	   Waters in the Gulf of Tonkin, Parcel
	   Is., Spratly Is.) [Active]
	Not claimed: LAOS (historical) [Active]
	[No dispute with Kampuchea claimed]

YEMEN ARAB REPUBLIC	DEMOCRATIC YEMEN (Northern and Eastern borders, oil discovery) [Active] Not claimed: SAUDI ARABIA (Border

COUNTRY	DISPUTES
	undemarcated) [Passive]
YUGOSLAVIA	None claimed ALBANIA (Kosovo) [Active]
ZAIRE	No response ZAMBIA [Presidents agreed to settle boundary dispute March 1981]
ZAMBIA	ZAIRE [Presidents agreed to settle boundary dispute March 1981]
ZIMBABWE	None claimed

INDEX

Aegean Sea, 26, 43, 73, 76,
    93-100, 121, 126, 128
Aguiar, Dias de, 88, 90
Antarctic, 101-114, 125
    American Antarctic, 105
    Claimant States, 106
    Consultative Committee, 105,
        109, 111
    Mineral Regime, 109, 110
    Nature Park, 102, 108
    Superpowers, 111, 112
    Third world, 105, 112
    Treaty, 106
    UK-Argentina clash, 112
Alto Adige, see South Tyrol
Arbitration, 41, 42, 73, 75,
    82, 85, 88, 101
Archipelagic Regime, 108
Arctic, 101, 102, 104, 107,
    108
    Northwest Passage, 108
Argentina, see Beagle Channel
    and Falkland Islands case
    studies
    See also Arctic, Antarctic

Balkans, 15
Barbarians, 5, 9, 12, 13, 17
Base-line, definition of, 25
Bargaining, 35-36, 132
    Disaggregation of issues,
        129
    Interest vs. positional, 37,
        132
    Meta-game, 36
    Style, 36
Barkun, Michael, x
Beagle Channel, 71-77
Beeby draft, see Antarctic,
    mineral regime
Blainey, Geoffrey, 33, 120
Border, viii, 117
    Agreements, 6
    Case studies, xi

Closed border policy, 17
Conflict, 31ff.
    Data, 26, Appendix I
    Stages, 30-32
    Escalation, 25, 29
    Taxonomy for disputes, 25-26
Boundary, vii, 3, 8, 13, 117
    Astronomical, 14
    Disputes, positional, 2, 18,
        25
    Administration of, 5
    Exchanges mediated, viii, 4,
        5, 9, 10, 11, 13, 31, 122
    Imperial, 6, 12
    Natural, 5, 10
Blocs, 19, 28, 29, 30
Brezhnev, Leonid, 68
Brussels Communique, 94, 95
Buffer States, 4, 14, 16
Burton, Richard Sir, 63
Butterworth, R.L., 26-28
Byrnes, James, 69

Caesar, 13
Cairo Declaration, 67, 69
Carter, Jimmy, 79
Case studies, 49-114
    Arctic & Antarctic, 101-114
    Argentina-Chile (Beagle
        Channel), 71-77
    Ecuador-Peru, 85-91
    Ethiopia-Somalia, 59-64
    Falkland/Malvinas, 51-58
    Greece-Turkey (Aegean Sea),
        93-100
    Japan-USSR (Northern
        Territories), 79-84
    US-Canada (Gulf of Maine),
        79-84
Camp David, 37
Canada, see case studies
    Arctic & Antarctic,
    Gulf of Maine
Cenepa River, 87-90

Center-Periphery, see
    Boundary, exchanges
Ch'in, 12
China, 8-9, 12, 15, 25, 44,
    111
    see also Empire, Chinese
Chile, see Beagle Channel
Colonies, 6, 14, 15
Commodus, 13
Condor range, 88, 90
Conflict, ix-x, 4-6, 31-38,
    117, 120-126
Contadora, 127
Continental Shelf, 4, 20, 25,
    81-82, 95, 97, 107, 118
    Cases: North Sea, 97
    Channel islands, 97
    Libya-Tunisia, 96, 98
Curzon Line, 3

Demirel, Suleyman, 93
Deutsch, Karl, 30
Divortium Aquarum, 88, 90-91
Djinghis Khan, 7
Dufek Intrusion, 102
Duress, 88

Ecuador, see Ecuador-Peru case
    study
Ellsmere island, 107
Empire:
    British, 16, 17
    Chinese, 8
    Roman, 5, 11-12
    Imperial relations, 6, 11
Estoppel, 75
Equidistance principle, 79,
    81-82, 107, 132
Ethiopia, see Ethiopia-Somalia
    case study
Ex aequo et bono, 76, 98, 119

Face saving, 133
Falkland islands, vii, 3, 34-
    35, 102, 105, 120-121,
    131
    See also Case study
Feudalism, 11-12
Fisher, Roger, 37, 125
Fitzroy, Robert, 71, 74

Frontier, viii, 5, 11, 15, 17
Functionalism, 129

Geophysical year, 106
Germany, 33, 38, 126
GIUK gap, 101
Glomar Challenger, 102
Gran, Ahmed, 59, 63
Great Wall, 11-12
Greece, see Aegean Sea case
    study
Gulf of Maine, see case study

Haile Selassie, 61
Hall, Duncan, 15
Hegemonic power, 30
Hitler, Adolf, 34
Hongkong, 131

Icebergs, 106
Information gathering, 124
International Court of Justice
    (ICJ), 25, 81-82, 93, 95,
    97-98, 118, 120, 132
Islands, legal effect, 97-98

Japan, see Northern
    Territories case study
Jefferson, Thomas, 14

Kerguelen, Josephe de, 105
Kissinger, Henry, 129

Lamaism, 7-8
Lattimore, Owen, 7, 11-12
Luard, 112
Luhmann, Niklas, 10

Magellan Straits, 71, 74
Mandel, Robert, 28-30
Manchu dynasty, 9
McMahon line, 14
Median principle, 82
Mediation, 39, 42, 119, 127
    Papal, 73, 120
    US-Brazil-Argentina, 85
Menelik II, 59-60, 62-63
Mineral soups, 104
Modus vivendi, 126
Mongols, 5-9

156

Mussolini, Benito, 61
Nationalism, 3
Neutrality, 4, 14
Neutral zone, 16
Nomads, 7
Northern Territories, see
    Japan-USSR case study
Northwest Passage, see Arctic

OAS, 42, 127
OAU, 42, 62-63
Oceanic principle, 71, 73-75,
    119
Orellana, Francisco de, 87
Osborn, Earl, v

Perceptions, 117-122
    Congruence of, 123, 125
Peru, see Ecuador-Peru case
    study
Pizarro, Gonzales, 85, 87, 89
Postdam Agreement, 67-68
Powers:
    Great Powers, 4, 33
    Small Powers, 33
Poirier, Pascal, 105
Principles (legal), 118-120,
    123, 127-128, 132-133
Protectorate, 14
Protocol of Rio, see Treaty of
Prudhoe Bay, 102

Regimes, 19, 26
    See also Antarctica
Richardson, L.F., 30
Rights, 4, 6-7
    Unbundling of, 26, 130
    See also Sovereignty,
        Territory
Roosevelt, Franklin, 34, 68
Ross Sea, 102
Russia, 9
    See also Soviet Union

Saar issue, 38
Sakhalin, 65-66, 68-69
Sadat, Anwar, 129
Sayyid, Muhammad, 61
Sectoral principle, 105, 107
Shuttle diplomacy, 125
Sinai, 37

Singer, David, 30
Sinkiang, 9
Social formation, 7, 17
Society, 7
Somalia, see Ethiopia-Somalia
    case study
Sovereignty, 11, 129-130
South Tyrol (Alto Adige), 38,
    130-131
Special Circumstances Rule,
    81-82, 99, 107
Spheres of:
    Influence, 6, 14-15
    interest, 14-15
Spitzbergen (Svaalbard), 107,
    131
Stalin, 9
State system, 4-6, 11
Soviet Union, 33, 101, 107,
    126
    Japan, see Japan-USSR case
        study
    Yugoslavia, 126
    Antarctica, 43, 126
    Europe, 33, 38
Suzerainty, 4, 6, 9, 61

Terra nullius, 4, 54
Territory, 3, 9, 25, 75
    Division, 14
    Fixed property in, 8
    Title to, viii
    Tribal, 7-8
    Rights, 6, 25
Third parties:
    Intervention, vii
    Implicit-explicit, ix, 38-42
    Role in settlement of
        disputes, ix, 26, 57,
        122-125
Timasheff, Nicholas, 32
Treaty, Garcia-Herrera (1890),
    85
    Of Arbitration between
        Argentina and Chile
        (1902), 73
    Commerce, Navigation and
        Delineation between
        Russia and Japan (1885),
        65
    Madrid (1670), 53

Peking (1860), 9
Portsmouth (1905), 65
Puerto Montt (1978), 73
Guayaquil (1929), 85
the Pyrenees (1659), 11
Washington (Antarctica)
   (1959), 101, 106
Rio (Protocol) (1942),
   87-88
San Francisco (1951), 65
Tordesillas (1493), 53
Uccielli (1887), 59
Trieste, 38, 126
Trudeau, Elliot, 79
Turkey, see Aegean Sea case
   study

Ultra vires, 73
United Nations (UN), 42, 106
  Mission, questionnnaire vii,
     Appendix I
  Secretary General, 42
  Security Council, 95, 98
  General Assembly, 111
United Nations Conference on
   Law of the Sea (UNCLOS
III), 99, 105, 107, 109,
   111
United Kingdom, 34-35
  Clash with Argentina, 44
  See Empire, British
  See also Falkland and Beagle
     Channel case studies
United States, 19, 28, 87,
   107, 126
  Arctic & Antarctica, 102,
     106, 110-112
  Canada, 19, 42, 118-121, 132
  See also Gulf of Maine case
     study
  Mediation, 28, 42, 69
Uti Possidetis, 53, 71, 73,
   75, 85, 89-90, 119

War, 117
  Persian, 34
  Algeria, 34
  World War II, 33-35
  See also Conflict
Ward, Kingdon, 10

Yalta, 67-69

ABOUT THE AUTHORS

Friedrich Kratochwil teaches International Law and International Relations at Columbia University. He is the author of International Order and Foreign Policy (1978), and co-editor with Richard Falk and Saul Mendlowitz of International Law: A Contemporary Perspective (1985).

Paul Rohrlich is an Assistant Professor at the University of Vermont. He received his Ph.D. from Columbia University. He has contributed to several journals, such as Journal of International Affairs and International Journal of Intercultural Relations.

Harpreet Mahajan is a Ph.D. candidate in the Department of Political Science, Columbia University. She holds a doctorate from Jawaharlal Nehru University, India, and is the author of Arms Transfers to India, Pakistan and the Third World (1982).